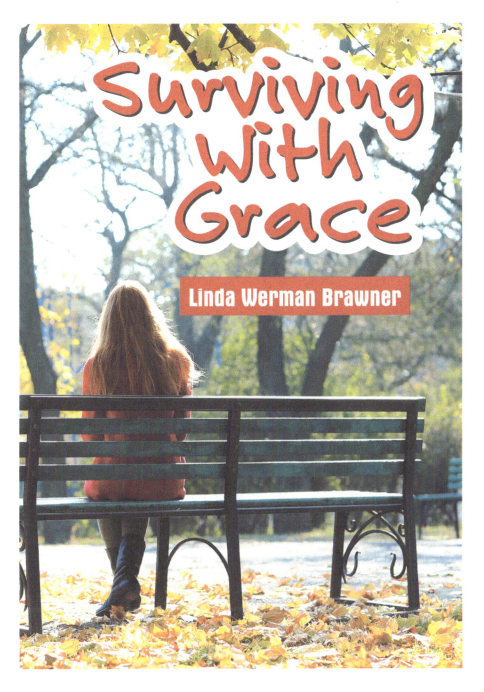

Surviving With Grace

Linda Werman Brawner

TEACH Services, Inc.
P U B L I S H I N G
www.TEACHServices.com • (800) 367-184

Copyright © 2015 Linda Werman Brawner
Copyright © 2015 TEACH Services, Inc.

ISBN-13: 978-1-4796-0511-8 (Paperback)
ISBN-13: 978-1-4796-0512-5 (ePub)
ISBN-13: 978-1-4796-0513-2 (Mobi)

Library of Congress Control Number: 2015936516

Unless otherwise noted, Scripture quotations are from the New American Standard Bible, copyright © 1960, 1962, 1963, 1968, 1971, 1972, 1973, 1975, 1977, 1994 by the Lockman Foundation. Used by permission.

Published by

TEACH Services, Inc.
P U B L I S H I N G
www.TEACHServices.com • (800) 367-1844

Dedication

I dedicate this book to my family, living and dead. To my parents, you taught me to value hard work. To my husband, you loved me unconditionally. To my daughter, we did it. We turned a horrible, painful time into a powerful witness of God's great love for all of us. To my grandchildren, heed the words in part two. They will protect you from so much harm.

Contents

Part 1

The Courage to Say Goodbye

Chapter 1

Sometimes I wear widowhood like a badge of honor. The first few weeks were easy because relief swept in like a tide smoothing a sandy beach. The hardest part was telling Kelly, our daughter. Like the unrelenting tide, I repeatedly, gently assured her that Daddy was indeed gone. Her gull-like cries of denial pierced my heart.

Her grief would be her own battle. All I could offer was this piece of advice: "Don't be strong for me. Be Kelly. God will be strong for both of us." In the last year or so, we've made a safe little family of two, sharing our sorrows, sharing our concerns, and taking turns coddling the other. Sometimes I have trouble remembering that she is just sixteen.

*****

Mother's Day night he went to bed struggling to breathe, more so than usual. I spent the afternoon asking God if I should send him to the hospital. I listened for His voice with every fiber of my being, but I heard nothing. God's silence didn't worry me.

At bedtime I sat next to him on the couch where he usually slept. I knew he would spend the night sitting up. I wrapped an arm around his shoulder and prayed out loud, asking God to be with him through the night. I had never done that before. Jerry didn't respond in any way. All this was about normal for a weekend because he had gone an extra day without dialysis. I kissed his forehead and went to bed at 10 p.m. He always insisted I get my sleep no matter what might lay ahead in the night. I assured myself that he couldn't die on Monday because I had so many things to do.

In the middle of the night I woke up. I could hear his breathing above the oxygen concentrator. I fell back asleep, assuring myself that he would be all right. At seven o'clock I awoke and said my prayers. At 7:11 a.m. I passed the microwave on my way to the living room. I couldn't hear him breathing. His skin felt no colder than usual, and his body wasn't stiff. I called 911 and told the dispatcher that I thought he was dead. I put on a robe and waited for the paramedics. I quickly phoned Terry's house. I needed to tell her son that I couldn't give him a ride to school.

The day had finally come.

Jerry had been sick almost three years, and I was prepared for this day. I wanted to scream "Don't bring him back. His struggle is over." when the medics brought in a defibrillator. They took one look and made no attempt. Instead, they called the funeral home. They waited until an elderly friend, David, came to help me. At the drop of a hat, he spent most of the day with us.

The first thing on our agenda was to inform Kelly who was at boarding school forty-five minutes away. A staff member called to inform me that several in the dorm already knew. Bad news travels like wildfire, scorching as it spreads. Terry had called her girls. The dean slipped a do not disturb sign on Kelly's door and that gave me time to tell her face-to-face. I focused on duties and on carrying myself with dignity.

God had carried us thus far, and I was determined that my conduct would reflect my faith. I focused on comforting our friends and making it easy for them to express their condolences. I learned that if I didn't like what they had to say, I could clutch them to my shoulders and let their words roll off my back. They too needed to mourn and helping is one way to express grief. I tried to find a job for everyone who offered to help. I tried to make it fit their talents and availability.

Late that evening the pastor called. He would be tied up with doctoral classes all week. I told him I wanted to have calling hours on Thursday at the church and postpone the memorial service until the next week when he would be available. He had so faithfully visited Jerry that I couldn't imagine letting a total stranger conduct the service. The pastor needed closure too. I summoned the courage to tell him I would do a eulogy.

"I really don't think you should do that," he replied.

I neither backed down nor asserted myself. He knew the stress I had been under. I knew he wanted to protect me from more than I could bear.

The next day an elder called. Ken gently discouraged me from speaking.

"Ken, many from church didn't make the time to visit Jerry. It was too hard for them to watch someone their own age die. Jerry wasn't a tidy little Christian. I need to assure them that he knew Jesus loved him." I launched into a story about Jerry.

When I finished, Ken simply answered, "And you will do that." His confidence settled the question.

I offered to speak from a manuscript so that the pastor could take over if I fell apart. I knew I wouldn't, but he didn't.

Jerry made no funeral arrangements. He felt it would just hasten the day. He did get his business affairs in order so that we could enjoy the time we had left. I had made the decision to speak six months before Jerry's death when it looked as if it was imminent. I wrote parts of it in my head, but never set anything down on paper. Perhaps I too was afraid of hastening the day.

The eulogy was one of the finest things God and I ever did. The gold of faith, of complete trust, shone through our black, black night. In the sanctuary I placed a large acrylic portrait of the Brawner family. As I approached the pulpit, I studied it thoughtfully for a moment. I nodded approval and then from the pulpit said, "That's a fine looking family. I would be proud to call them my own. Oh! They are." I then launched into Jerry's story.

Jerry loved to watch movies. That was one of the first things I learned about him. If his life were a movie, this would be the part where the credits roll by. There would be the list of stars and then the producer, God, and the director, Jesus Christ. The Holy Spirit would be in charge of properties and an endless list of angels would make up the behind the scenes crew.

When I stepped on the scene in 1986, Jerry's life became a romantic comedy. Ohio isn't noted for big quakes, but the day before we met there was one in Geauga County that I felt clear down in Ashland. Prior to the quake, I had been brushing my hair and talking to the Lord about my singleness. "I'm too stubborn and set in my ways. I will just make some man miserable." Poor Jerry. At times I made him miserable, but still we grew closer and closer together.

The courtship consisted of us falling steadily in like. This disappointed him so much that he finally asked me if I could be more romantic, or "mushy" if you will. I gave him a tiny jar of cornmeal. Thus began the laughter that bound us together. He taught Kelly and me to laugh in the tight corners.

Our most memorable date was when we decided to canoe on the Clear Fork on Sabbath afternoon. We dumped once and lost a paddle. I was downstream from the canoe and pushed against it. Jerry assured me that he had the canoe, to just let it float over me. "Are you nuts?" I asked while my eyebrows dripped. "I don't want to get my face in this." The trip got worse. When I spotted the paddle, I literally stepped out of the canoe. Jerry calmly said, "Oh my," as he fell in the opposite direction. I fell through the glassy smooth water. I seized the paddle and somehow we got our drenched bodies aboard. In the parking lot, we decided that canoeing was entirely too much work for Sabbath.

Jerry never proposed to me. We just started planning the wedding. We were married April 5, 1987. It had been a mild winter, but on April 4 the snow came down. It was almost as if God was housecleaning. "Oops! Gotta get rid of this." All the weddings on that day were cancelled but the sun was shining and the pavement cleared for our celebration. It symbolized our future together. Every time things looked rough, the Son would shine forth and show us the way.

Kelly popped into our lives almost as quickly as we figured out what causes those things. From the time she was tiny, she learned gentleness and kindness from her daddy. When she was hurt or upset and just wailing away, Jerry was the mother for he excelled in comforting others. As she grew she increased in the gentle strength she saw in him. Kelly and I both had an easy time of helping him because he always considered our needs and encouraged us to take time to enjoy the things he couldn't.

He taught us to weave humor into the hard times. I often shared his dinner at the hospital—except when the tray was labeled "renal diet." That is the worst food known to the industrialized world, and it usually drove me to smuggling contraband so that we both could survive his stay. Last Christmas was the best Christmas I can remember. He was in the hospital and that slowed things down enough for me to enjoy Jerry and Kelly. The three of us hoarded the holiday. Christmas Eve Kelly and I dragged in all the gifts and some Taco Bell. We laughed about nothing and treasured the moments. In the morning we smuggled in brunch. In a big thermos I brought the best hot chocolate I ever had.

Jerry wasn't much of a burden during his illness. Even if it meant struggling and straining, he always did as much for himself as possible. When fatigue was getting the best of me, he would find a movie on TV that appealed to my tastes. The day before he died, he tried to get me started on a movie so that I would put my feet up and rest. Then he would doze off and I would enjoy the program because Jerry wanted me to.

The Christmas before he started to weaken, I myself was in poor health and quite despondent. Despite bitter cold we went to an evening movie. I was bundled up so tightly I could hardly move, and yet I complained, "I am so cold. I am so cold. Even my heart is cold." As he laid his bare hand on my glove I knew he was the only one on earth that understood my cold heart. Even as he weakened, I could count on him to hold me and rub my back. He always offered tenderness and affection and support. Some say I've had a hard life lately. It would have been a lot more difficult if Jerry hadn't loved me so well. (I noticed the women getting teary-eyed at this statement.)

He knew his way around the kitchen. He made the best Swedish pancakes in the world. He always liked to cook now and then. One day he hobbled out to the kitchen in his walker. He grabbed my blender and made an omelet. Just whipped up eggs milk and button mushrooms. The final product was a pasty shade of gray. As he slowly munched on it he said, "You know, if you had made this I wouldn't touch it." (The men grinned. They knew exactly what Jerry meant.)

Almost two years ago, Jerry's movie became action adventure as we adjusted to his varying levels of strength. On the anniversary of his open-heart surgery, a heart catheterization warned us that there was more trouble, and it couldn't be fixed. Just before we left the hospital, the family doctor warned me that he didn't have more than several years, and he could just suddenly go. I never told Jerry because he pretty well knew it. I went through the countryside as I took him home. One thing bugged me. "Jerry, you never proposed to me. You promised you would someday."

"Linda, will you marry me?"

"Yes."

"Why?"

"Because I love you very, very much." I gripped the steering wheel tightly.

"That's not good enough."

I looked over and saw mischief in his eyes. I grinned softly. "Because you have one foot in the grave and the other on loose dirt."

"Yes!" he grinned.

"But you're not rich." We drew strength from our laughter.

Jerry didn't suffer constantly, but at times he suffered greatly. He rarely complained, and he never blamed God. One night in the emergency room he suffered especially hard. As I searched his eyes, I could see Jesus on the cross. Jerry's trials drew him upward.

Jerry's movie was laced with hope and laughter and under girded with courage and holy strength. Coming to planet earth soon will be the glorious sequel. It stars Jesus Christ and a cast of millions rising in the air to meet Him. (I gestured toward the stained glass window in our church that depicts that scene.)

Come quickly, Lord Jesus.

Chapter 2

Today's my father's birthday. He died in 1998. I had such a hard time trusting God once Papa died. I think it had to do with his deathbed request: "Linda, if your family is to amount to anything, you have to take charge of it."

Papa taught me many useful things, but this was bad advice. With those parting words, I lost respect for Jerry and forgot that God provides for us. This doesn't mean that we don't work and do our best to support our families; it means we don't have the strain of thinking everything is up to us. When I look back on my life since I moved away from home into my own apartment, I never really stood on my own. As I helped those I could, others helped me. I never could be tight fisted with someone in need because God was never tight fisted with me.

About a year after Papa died, I cracked under the strain. I was so busy thinking I had to do everything all by myself that I had alienated myself from Jerry and stopped taking antidepressants. I kept God in a distant corner of my mind. The more frightened I grew on the inside, the more I tried to make the outside look good. Finally, the fall before Jerry's open-heart surgery, I couldn't do it anymore. I was so far gone from physical exhaustion that it took a long time to get better.

The breakdown was a miserable time for me. I have this theory that all mental illness can be traced to guilt—false guilt or deserved. I suppose it is simplistic because it doesn't take into account what are called brain disorders—actual malfunctions of our gray matter. My own depression is a chemical imbalance.

Jerry and I rarely spent time apart, but when I went to see the psychiatrist, he was in Washington State seeing his foster brother. It spooked him that I got so bad. "I knew something was the matter, but I didn't know what to do for you. I'll do anything to make you happy."

God can give us such clarity when it seems as if we have no brains left. "Jerry, you can't make me happy. You can only love me." Jerry never felt worthy of my love. Somehow these words set his heart at ease. He spent more time hugging me and holding my hand. Not even God can make us happy. If we are determined to complain and whine, it doesn't matter what wondrous things He does for us. We could have every material thing we set our hearts on, have great health, and have happy and healthy loved ones. None of this does any good if we are determined to be sorrowful. Once Jerry understood that I didn't expect him to make me happy, he was free to love me.

In the blackness prior to getting help, all I could think about was killing myself. I never realized how much I thought of it until the doctor asked me if I had a plan. I did. It was a well-thought-out plan, and that scared me. Generally I succeed when I put that much thought into a project.

I can't say why I wanted to kill myself. Christ had gotten me through enough scrapes that I didn't doubt His ability to help me cope with the loss of my father and other loved ones who had died or moved away at that time. I was just weary of the pain. Every time I turned around, there was a new loss or hardship to deal with. I had no good reason. Sin never makes sense. When it starts to make sense, you are on dangerous ground.

In the blackness I learned a priceless lesson. Christ stands right by our side all the time, even if we don't know Him or acknowledge Him at all. He is eager to comfort us and to heal us. I had been taught that God is holy and cannot bear the presence of sin. Christ is God. He made everything mentioned in Genesis. He was with His people when Moses led them out of Egypt, as the fiery pillar by night and the cloud by day.

When He took on human form, He mingled with us in our vileness and laid down His life in order to have the right to rescue us from sin. He knows all of our dirtiness, and yet He still loves us. He is able to picture us restored or healed from all of the effects of sin. He does not step back when we sin. Our sin just makes it hard or impossible to see Him.

As I came out of that black, black depression, I realized that since I am so well loved by God I can afford to call my mistakes sin. I can afford to say, "This was wrong, Lord. Where do we go from here?" It is so much easier to see the solution to your problems when you aren't fussing over what a screw up you are and how terrible this is. We cannot possibly make such a terrible mess that Christ can't untangle it. Sometimes it take years, but He does fix us. It's been five years since my breakdown, and only now am I really well and strong.

I frightened most people at church. Depression is often mistaken for tossing away one's faith. They stood back and assumed the worst. I didn't have the energy to chase after them. A visit or a phone call would have helped so much. You don't have to understand in order to love. While friends cannot replace mental health professionals, the pros don't replace friends either. If I had broken my leg, a deacon would have opened the door for me instead of hovering in the background waiting for a professional. Since I broke my mind, they stood back and prayed.

It seemed as if they didn't step forward as a church until Jerry died. But maybe their help at the time was simply more visible. Mental health is a scary business because it is harder to say, "This can't happen to me." Folks underestimate the importance of light and bright. I would have appreciated the distraction of a few wholesome jokes or a pretty card reminding me that the sender was praying. I would have loved it if people took the time to tell me how God was blessing them. When life gets that black, the little glimmers of hope shine very brightly. No one can fix you when you are depressed. Professionals can help provide a healing environment with medication, talk therapy, and suggestions on how to improve one's coping skills. God can comfort and give you every tool you need to get well, but a body has to pick up the tools and go to work. You learn to praise yourself for every small step you make toward wholeness. If you want to get well, you focus on what is right in your life. Usually that means beginning with God who is the author of every good and perfect gift.

This chronicle may seem like a continuous patting myself on the back, but the glory goes to my Savior. In my constant amazement at what He has done for and through me, I sometimes seem a little full of myself. I know how black and evil I can be. I pray that no one thinks I am saying, "Look at me! I have arrived at perfection." The study of our lives should be how to guard ourselves from temptation. None of us will arrive until He puts an end to sin.

In *The Mummy* Brendan Fraser fights one creepy creature after another—an endless stream of threats to his safety. As he hacks and punches, he looks into the camera and says, "Boy, this just keeps getting better and better." That describes my life from the death of my father until the death of my husband. One horror after another kept marching at me, and I no longer had the energy to be worried or afraid.

Seven months after my breakdown, Jerry had open-heart surgery—July 10, 2000. We both listened in horror as the doctor gave us the short version of the surgery. Jerry would have three, possibly more, bypasses replaced by pieces of the artery from an arm. His legs were too bad to be considered. In six days they would send him home, but since he did heavy lifting for his job, he would need to wait six months before returning to work, although the doctor said he would be better than ever then. I think he said something about sawing the breastbone and collapsing the lungs. When he left, Jerry cried, and I sat there trying not to vomit. That was a Friday, and the tenth was a Monday. They kept Jerry because he was in danger of having a heart attack, and it would be fatal if he were home. I was terrified. We had drifted apart, and now we were finding our way back to each other. If he had died then, the load of guilt would have been enormous.

On Monday I decided to wait at home rather than at the hospital. I had spent Sunday night with Jerry at the hospital. In the morning I kissed him goodbye when he went into surgery, and then I headed home. A number of friends waited with me at the house. This rubbed my nerves raw. Some of the friends left for the hospital. I figured I could pray better at home. "Lord, help us. Lord. Lord. Father. Lord." I was so frightened I couldn't string more than three words together, none of them a complete thought.

I stumbled numbly through each day, sensing how the prayers of our friends carried me. Prayer is more powerful than we can ever realize while we are on earth.

The surgery was just one more instance of life ripping the rug out from under me. Everything looked well. He was supposed to be on the breathing machine for twenty-four to thirty hours. A little less than twenty-four hours later they took him off the respirator. But twelve hours later they put him back on and kept him there for a total of five days. The brief time he was off, he hoarsely complained of being hot. Every ten minutes I changed the cool washcloth on his forehead so he wouldn't have to struggle to ask. I focused on this duty as a little scrap of sanity.

Saturday afternoon they took him off. I brought Kelly because she missed her daddy. She was twelve at the time. She and I saw so little of each other because when I wasn't working, I was at the hospital. A couple of days later she told me, "I was mad at you for not bringing me to the hospital sooner. Now I understand. You did the right thing."

I did what I could to shield her, but our family is small and so is our house. I had to inform her so that her imagination wouldn't run wild. I'm not sure the truth was less scary, but at least she could trust us. I thought Kelly raised herself that summer, but in reality the church stepped in so smoothly that I didn't notice the help. I loved her, but I just didn't have much left for her. I was lucky that she understood.

When Jerry came to, it was just the beginning of more horrors. His mind wasn't right. The physical therapist could make no progress in exercising his hand or getting him to do breathing exercises. He simply couldn't grasp the importance. His left arm never recovered, and he ended up on oxygen six months later. His struggling kidneys failed. The church joined me in praying, and in October he was able to stop dialysis. This gift gave us courage. Unfortunately, the following May he started up again, but we were thankful for the break.

His six days in the hospital turned into a month. I spent every spare moment by his side. One day he even let me take the bed because I was cold and weary, and he wanted me to linger awhile. One of the doctors walked in and did a double take. Luckily none of the nurses considered giving me his insulin.

Often I drove past beautiful green lawns and blue, blue skies on my way to the hospital. "It's still beautiful. It's still beautiful," I told God. The ability to notice this loveliness comforted me. God's fingers smoothed by hair and caressed my face in the form of a summer breeze. His tears fell as rain, cleansing my soul of hatred and anger and guilt. Always savor beauty for it draws us close to God.

I had so little control of my life that summer and following. Work was the only steady thing. I only missed one day, the day of his surgery. Most days I would ask Him to make sure I did what needed to be done. I often prayed through my work. Even on days when Jerry was relatively okay, I felt as if I couldn't organize my time. Still God did a great job of guiding me.

My one constant prayer was and is, "Help me hear Your voice." Most of those years my ear would fairly strain because I got so many answers in the trying times. For example, we owned a little too much to go on Medicaid. I was so fearful about the money. At the time, I didn't know the extent of his private disability insurance, and I worried how we would pay our portion of the bill. I was accustomed to always having enough and some to share. "Lord, help me to be able to give," was one of my prayers. Well, the hospital wrote off what we owed because our insurance was good. Disability insurance not only carried us through recovery, but it supplemented Jerry's social security disability. Even now, Kelly and I live on less than ever, but we still have enough and some to share. Jerry didn't leave us a great deal, but everything we own is ours free and clear, and we do have a small nest egg for emergencies.

At the time we had six thousand dollars in credit card debt that worried me. Then I realized that our tax-free disability was more than Jerry's take home pay. As a bonus, a sick husband can't shop, and so our debt dwindled to nothing by the time he passed away. We even had the house paid off.

In retrospect, I don't know why I was so worried about poverty. From the time I got my own place, I started to tithe, and God proved His faithfulness. A couple of years later, I more fully understood the concept. All we have is God's in the first place. Our health, our intellect, our strength, our ability to earn and save money—these are all gifts from Him. I never have been tight fisted with those in need because God has never been tight fisted with me. Tithing is a returning of ten percent and a way to show our trust in Him. Early in life I learned to consider Him my employer or boss. Businesses come and go, but God endures forever.

God taught me so many valuable things during Jerry's illness. I saw Him ably handle impossible problems. Some Christians talk of God closing doors and opening others. He caused a few doors to be slammed in my face, but He always gave us something better, something wonderful because it clearly came from His hand. His working was so wondrous that sometimes it seemed as if He didn't bother with new doors but simply punched a hole in the wall that we might escape the latest terror.

The most wondrous thing I learned was that God didn't need me to make Him happy. I pleased Him simply because I drew breath. I was saved simply because I asked Him. Relieved of the burden of pleasing Him, I was free to love Him, free to let Him shape me into a better person.

Chapter 3

We all handle grief differently. When I comfort people who are grieving, I listen and reassure them that they are normal. Their world has been ripped open. There is no one strategy for surviving. It is a wicked path, and only God can guide us through it. Oh, we all get angry with Him for one reason or another. In my case, I was just stunned how much it hurt once all the social obligations of grieving were over.

I had a hard time admitting I was angry with God. Instead, the anger randomly popped out in the most inappropriate ways. How could I be mad at God when He had taken care of so many of the details? It seemed supremely unfair to be angry at One who had carried us so well. Once I realized that I was angry because He didn't shield me from the pain of loss, I was okay. Sometimes we hide our anger from Him. We might as well get it off our chest because He already knows it is there. Go ahead and yell at God. He is always big enough to take it and not hold a grudge or be discouraged by our unfairness. God can't help us when we pretend everything is just fine.

I had a hard time remembering Jerry. It was my way of coping with the loss. For about six months I couldn't remember his voice or how soft his bald head was to the touch of my lips. I couldn't remember his smile, his careful smile that concealed his tooth shortage. His dry wit was delicious. I remember once. The house was dark and quiet as we lay in bed. He cracked some sort of political joke. I thought a moment and then the laughter spilled out of me like pure water from a spring. He held me tight and whispered, "You are the only person on this planet that would have gotten that joke." In time we grew to function as one mind.

How we met is an interesting story. An acquaintance had been nagging me to get married as if I could just pick up a man my size at Kmart. Heck, something that important and I would have splurged at Kaufman's. One night I told the Lord, "I'm going on 29. I would like to be engaged by the time I am 30." The next morning I got up, worked on some writing, and then packed up to go home to Willoughby. Just before I left, I brushed my hair in front of the mirror and told God, "I'm too old, too stubborn, and too set in my ways. I'll just make some man miserable." Bingo. On Sabbath I met the perfect man to make miserable. That was February 1, 1986.

I got along well with Jerry the day I met him because I thought he was married. When he introduced himself to me at a church dinner, he just gave me his first name. Since he was standing next to a woman named Karen Black, I assumed he was Mr. Black. We chatted wonderfully because I felt no need to make an impression.

By the time I figured out that he wasn't married, I knew I had made a great impression. I left the dinner making a mental note to break away more often to visit my parents. After all, the Bible promises blessings to those who honor their mother and father. I impressed him by chatting about a book project. He entertained me with a cockroach story. He served during the Vietnam War but never in combat. During his six months in Japan, he found a huge cockroach in his quarters. He promptly locked it up in a puzzle box. A week later he opened it, figuring the bug would be quite dead. As he peered into the box, the bug lunged at his face. *Aaaah!* I still laugh. Bugs don't scare me! Not as long as they keep a respectable distance from my face. Jerry taught me to savor the ten-year-old inside of me.

That night a mutual friend contacted me at my parent's house. We were all piqued with curiosity. Who would hunt me up at my parents' house? It turned out that Jerry wanted a date for the Valentine's banquet. On the day of the banquet, we were the only non-married couple, and I was the only girl wearing a real flower corsage. Thankfully our friends advised him not to buy silk. There is something wonderful about living petals and leaves from the Creator's hand.

The date seemed like a dud to Jerry. For me, this church was a home away from home, and I was so popular amongst the ladies that Jerry hardly saw me. I did sit by his side and eat and eat and eat. I had been too excited that day to eat, and my appetite caught up with me. Our mutual friend, Laura, had done all the cooking. She slid up behind us and asked Jerry, "Doesn't she eat like a bird?" Our eyes laughed while he politely agreed. In reality, I ate more like a Thanksgiving turkey who had no idea what lay ahead.

By spring Jerry moved to Ashland and got a job in Mansfield. We lived in separate apartments in the same building. It was an old house that had been divvied up. He had the attic, and my place was below his. My bedroom was originally some sort of sunroom. It had its own roof and seven windows. In fair weather it was like sleeping in a tree house. We delighted in telling people that although we shared a building we did not sleep under the same roof.

Jerry had a splendid cat named Clint. He was a large red point Siamese with dreamy blue eyes. He was quiet and a little skittish, a good-sized cat. We joked about fighting for custody if we ever broke up. I told my friends I would have married the cat if I could have found a tuxedo to fit. He was the only blue-eyed blond my husband would let me sleep with. His fur was thin and silky, so he loved to sleep under the covers.

As Jerry prepared to move to Ashland, I got to keep the cat. "Make sure he stays inside for a week so that he gets to know the place as his," he had told me. However, within twenty-four hours I had lost him. The windows had been shut and the door locked all day, so I figured he had to be in the apartment. That night I crawled into bed with a prayer on my lips. I noticed that the sheets felt warm. The little devil had crawled under the covers while I worked. I was relieved that he was safe. By the time Jerry and I were married and had a baby on the way, the cat and I frequently napped together. As I got large with child he learned to sleep behind me, near my shoulders. Ah. You haven't lived until you've had a purring heating pad.

The day I had Kelly, Clint and Jerry figured out I was in labor before I did. My hips hurt a lot toward the end. Around 1 a.m. I got up to use the bathroom. Every time I sat down on the bed, I got a sharp pain in my hips. I would rise and try to sit down again. I timed my sitting down with my contractions. I woke Jerry. It's a good thing I was healthy. When I didn't feel good, there was no rest for him. Jerry realized I was in labor and called the hospital. Clint ran back and forth on the carpet. HIs back was arched, his hair stood on end, and his claws ripped the rug with every gallop.

When we brought Kelly home from the hospital, Clint was a little scared of her. This little bundle that weighed almost as much as he did made such noise. I was so busy fussing with this bundle that I didn't even have time to nap with Clint. One day when my mom came to watch the baby, I grabbed Clint and we dove into bed together. He purred so loudly that I thought his little ribs would break. He had missed me. Eventually he learned the perks of having a baby—he would finish her bottles of formula. Once as she half-dozed in her walker, he gingerly stole a piece of homemade bread from her hand. He loved just about any food meant for the baby.

Clint and I only had words once over the baby. One evening I lay in bed reading for a few minutes. Clint had parked himself on my feet as if to say, "Mine!" Kelly was big enough to walk by holding on to the furniture. She was at the edge of the bed, possibly trying to pat the kitty. Kelly was a diplomat from day one. Her first word was kitty so Jerry and I wouldn't argue about whether it was Daddy or Mommy. Clint wanted his quality time, so he swatted her. This was where I started to pay attention. I took care of her little hand and then swatted him on the butt. "This is my kitten. You don't hurt her," I scolded.

A month later I was baking in the kitchen. As I concentrated on the recipe, I became dimly aware of a scuttling sound on the kitchen tile. Kelly was pulling Clint by the tail. I promptly scolded Kelly. If I wouldn't let Clint defend himself, I had better instruct Kelly in how to treat the cat.

See? I set out to help you picture Jerry, and I still have trouble remembering him—back to his story. He loved me and tried so hard not to be a burden. He remained as independent as possible. I can't remember how often he was hospitalized. Six? Eight times? Each time he was admitted through the ER and would remain there a terribly long time. Each time he would make sure I went home by ten or eleven at the latest. He knew I needed my sleep. At home he would struggle and strain to get out of a chair by himself even if I was right there. There were many times I hoisted him up by the back of his pants, but he knew that each time I didn't have to increased his chances of staying out of a nursing home.

The nursing home scene scared us both. There are many kind-hearted, hard working people employed in nursing homes. However, they are spread too thin, and a patient can't get the kind of attention they would from one able-bodied spouse who is available to help. God looked out for us. I didn't want Jerry in a nursing home. He would have died quickly just from his attitude toward those places. More and more they are becoming rehabilitation centers, but often they are a storage facility for the dying.

In October of 2002 Jerry spent a month in the hospital. He was weak as a kitten because he had truly been too sick to get out of bed. Two days before they released him I lost my job. I knew the place was going under, but I expected to be there through the end of the year. Instead I drew unemployment and became a full-time caregiver. I thanked God because I wanted to be by his side. The day I took him home, a nurse felt burdened to tell me that I couldn't take care of him. She assumed the toilet and bed at home were too low. I could understand her concerns. That visit they gave me a cot in his room because my back hurt so much. My hostility was clearly visible. A home study with hospital social workers would have helped. Telling me I wasn't equipped to take care of him as I wheeled him out the door was just plain stupid.

A couple of weeks later I got a friend in church to help me bring Jerry home from dialysis. I was exhausted and not much help in giving instructions. He hauled Jerry in like a sack of potatoes and made no effort to work with Jerry's abilities. His parting words were to encourage me to shelve Jerry in a nursing home. The next day I attended a memorial service for a man in our church. He had Alzheimer's and had died in a nursing home. His wife placed him there when she was no longer able to make sure he didn't wander off. He was happy as a lark, and she was able to visit him at mealtime to make sure he actually ate. It worked for them. At the service another friend swooped down on me. "You need to put him in a nursing home." I listened and tried to look as if I respected his words. These friends could see my strength failing. They knew Jerry was dying.

Their primary concern was that I still be left reasonably healthy. Jerry had become a vague idea in the back of their minds. I was a living, breathing sister who suffered before their eyes.

God honored my desire to keep Jerry at home. He died six months later. I was not a perfect wife, but I have no major regrets. God let Jerry go just before it got too difficult for us.

Chapter 4

God did so much to shelter Kelly, Jerry, and me. We could have gone bankrupt. We could have lost our faith. Kelly and I could be at odds. Jerry could have been mean and angry over his illness.

One thing that has been a great blessing is our biblical knowledge of God's character. Many in our circumstances struggle with why God allows suffering. Some even believe that He causes it. Suffering is the price of our freedom. God loves us so much that He is willing to allow us to choose not to follow Him. It would be terrible if we suffered alone because of our own sins and the sins of others. However, Jesus Christ so tenderly and thoroughly loves us that He not only suffered to redeem us from sin but He suffers with each and every one of us when we suffer. We never cry alone. He is right beside us. He never leaves our side even when fear and pain blind us to His presence. Focusing on the cross can help put our suffering in perspective. However, we should never let it trivialize our sufferings. Just because other people have it worse doesn't make our suffering less real or less valid. God has a harder time comforting us when we pretend we don't hurt. He cannot heal or restore His image in us if we pretend nothing is the matter.

Just before I became a Christian I had Christians praying for me. That frightened me. I'm independent. I wasn't going to conform to the social norms of any church. I still don't. It sounded creepy to be molded or transformed into the image of Christ. I pictured a shelf full of statues of Jesus—each shaped and painted identical to the others.

But I learned that in Christ there is freedom. If we sin, we are forgiven. If we repent, He will show us how to break free of our sins. He will work with us tirelessly, never condemning us. What happens when you take a prat fall in high school? Everyone laughs. If you are lucky, someone helps you up and says something to make you feel better. When we fall into sin, many laugh at us and some are deeply wounded. Jesus helps us up and says, "I still love you. I will help you fix what you have broken." He mends hearts and lives. When He carries us, we accomplish more than we thought possible—just the fact that I am alive and writing this proves my point.

Why did man sin in the first place? We had it so cushy in the Garden of Eden. This is where our buddy Satan comes in. Our planet wasn't the first thing God created. I have no idea how many worlds He created before He made ours. I do know that there were angels in heaven. One of them, Lucifer, had a high position—he was head of the angels, next in line to Jesus Christ. No created being could go higher than that. He had looks, talents, intelligence, and power. He only wanted one more thing— to be like God. Like all of God's creatures, he had freedom. He coveted the power of Jesus to speak things into being. He felt it was unfair that God would not give him this power. He stirred up heaven, and a third of the angels took his side. God loved Lucifer tenderly and thoroughly. He suffered when Lucifer suffered. He wanted to help Lucifer. He longed to say, "I still love you. I will help you fix what you have broken."

But Lucifer liked things broken and liked to see the angels arguing. After planet earth was made, he tempted Eve who disobeyed God. Adam couldn't picture life without Eve, and he couldn't picture a God big enough to restore Eve, so he joined her in sin. The finger pointing and arguing began. We have had almost seven thousand years of this discord— wars, famines, plagues, floods, and pestilence. Every evil can be traced to God giving His creation the freedom to choose whom they would serve. The price is horrific—the potential for good beyond our wildest dreams.

One common myth in Christianity is that if we have enough faith God will heal us or prosper us. Apparently true believers are never sick or poor. That's a load I refuse to live under. A few months before Jerry died a friend from church came to visit. He had the answer to our sufferings. If we would pray just so, God would heal Jerry. He brought a book from a denomination that believes Christ is a benevolent and impersonal force. He described the wondrous healings he experienced in regards to common aches and pains.

The formula is quite simple: Just ask God to heal you that you might serve Him. In essence, He is a small God. Just put your quarters in the vending machine and push the right buttons, and you will get what you want. If you get the wrong treat, it is your fault. Perhaps you cursed the dog or forgot to ask His forgiveness for gossiping. Following this logic, your suffering is strictly your own fault, and it is up to you to figure out the right coinage and the right buttons to get the desired blessing. The next question is who sinned? Was it Jerry or Kelly or me? Let's not forget to blame Jerry's parents. Under this theory, there is plenty of blame to go around.

I struggled for composure when our visitor dropped this on us. I asked, "If it is God's will to heal everyone immediately, what about the people we have met in the hospital and the opportunities we have had to share the gospel? " What about the people who strengthened our faith at those times? I was so proud when Jerry took over.

"What about the sovereignty of God? It is not always His will to heal, but He does know what is best for us."

It is easy to resign to the will of God when we are warm and safe and comfortable. Try saying it when you are tethered to an oxygen machine and struggling for every breath. Try believing it when your bodily fluids build up to the point where you are in constant and terrible pain. Try proclaiming it when you are staring death in the face. This is what it means to be a Christian—to trust God with your very life and to recognize His sovereignty, His right to rule.

We are here on this earth, and we suffer because God needs to establish His right to rule before He can put an end to sin forever. Like many, I long to see that end. However, if He ends it too soon, many will serve out of fear. Fear eventually leads to rebellion, and then it will start over in another garden somewhere in the universe. In the meantime, fear hinders our individuality.

What does it mean to be like Christ? It means loving those around us and growing more thoughtful of their needs and keeping His commandments by His strength and not our own. As we grow into the realization that we cannot earn His love and acceptance because we already have it, we are free to love Him. When we are free to love Him, there is no end to what we can accomplish. Christians aren't molded figurines. We are as varied and beautiful as the lilies of the field. We are fearfully and wonderfully made by a God who revels in variety.

Jerry suffered without blaming God. When in extreme pain, he certainly got grumpy. But I never once heard him ask, "Why me, Lord?" He understood that suffering is common to man. When we suffer without blaming God, we glorify Him.

It is always God's will to heal, but that doesn't mean that everyone will be healed on this earth. Some have to wait until resurrection morning when there will not be one flawed body or broken heart. All the injustices we suffer will be cheap enough for the glory we attain on that day. The memory of all the evil we have endured will fade in the brightness of His presence.

Chapter 5

Death is not a mystery. The Bible often describes it as a sleep, a blessed respite from life's trials. Jerry took comfort in the thought of a long, restful sleep before our Lord awakes us to a new, sinless life.

Does it matter what happens when we die? It sure does because what we believe about this subject reflects on the character of God—His holy, loving character that was attacked by Lucifer in heaven. Is God fair? Does He really love us?

Before I studied the Bible, the concept of an everlasting hell bothered me. How could a loving God enjoy roasting people forever? Only a divine power could keep us alive in hellfire. Why would He do that? Wouldn't this mean He couldn't destroy sin forever? Is sin more powerful than God? Cain killed Abel. Hitler was responsible for the death of millions. If the popular concept of going straight to heaven or hell were true, then Cain would roast roughly 5,000 years longer than Hitler. Is that fair? Is that merciful? We make jokes about hell—people there getting coffee breaks and other nonsense. However, the common teachings describe it as a place of extreme torment where the suffering is immeasurable. God is always amongst His creation. To say that He is the creator of such a place is to say that God embraces evil.

Our hell is here on this earth, and fortunately it doesn't last for-ever. Here we suffer, not for the sake of suffering, but that we might choose freely whom we shall serve. Here our suffering can make us like Christ if we mumble "help me" in prayer. Here our suffering can be a tool to help us share God with others. Jerry, Kelly, and I are proof that it takes so little to be saved by a God who will move heaven and earth in order to rescue us from sin. He desires that none should perish (John 3:16). He does not accomplish that by creating a place where the wicked can live forever.

When we die, we sleep in the grave. This is our lot regardless of the choices we make. Soon Christ will gather up the living and the dead who have trusted Him. Those who want nothing to do with Him and are alive at the time will simply die. At a later time those who would be unhappy liv-ing with Christ forever will be resurrected and destroyed with eternal fire. They will not burn forever, but the result of their death will be forever.

This flies in the face of popular teachings. Some so cherish the idea that those who have wronged them will suffer immeasurably for their sins that they cannot let go of the belief in an everlasting hell. This is spiteful. This is way beyond petty. I would rather my enemy come to know the joys of trusting God for everything. If he does this, he is no longer my enemy. I can afford to forgive him because Christ will make everything right when He returns for us.

We can afford to argue with God and ask Him questions. We do not have to fear Him in the sense of thinking He will arbitrarily send us to hell because He didn't like what we had to say. We do not have to agree with God constantly nor please Him in all things. If we accept that God died for our failings, we can trust Him in all things, including helping us to understand His ways. I can only gain by dialoging with Him. The Bible makes it clear that He is anxious that none should perish. Suffering is the price of freedom. Suffering has the potential of helping us to understand God.

Jerry always underestimated his worth. He had trouble believing that God really loved him and was willing to save him by His death on the cross. When illness forced him to go on disability, he had the time and energy to read the Bible for himself. As he grew weaker, that weakness gave me opportunities to show God's love while the pastor shared truths with him from the Bible. I honestly believe that if Jerry had been mirac-ulously healed I would not look forward to meeting him on resurrection morning. Yes, he was a good man. He was gentle and kind. I just don't think he would have placed his trust in God. We had hundreds of people praying for him. If it had been God's will to miraculously heal Jerry, it would have happened. However, God will always place our eternal good above our immediate needs when there is a conflict between the two. He wants us happy, whole, and well for eternity, not just for the here and now. We can face death with hope when we are confident of seeing our loved ones again.

I must explain the importance of prayer. In the book of Job, Satan accused God of being unfair. "You bless those who choose to serve You. You fill their lives with every good thing. You spoil and pamper them so they wouldn't dream of living Your side." That was the gist of Satan's accusation. And with that, God allowed Satan to test Job so that the universe could see that God's children follow Him through the good and bad times. He does not coerce us to obey Him with favors. When believers suffer and remain faithful, we show the universe that He is worthy of our devotion simply because He is God. When we suffer without blaming Him, we glorify God. We declare that He alone is the Author of all that is good.

So why do we pray? First, God invites us to ask Him for anything. Prayer is not some incomprehensible formula of words. Prayer is talking to God as a friend. The more friends talk, the better they understand one another. Next, God doesn't interfere with our lives. If we ask for His help, we give Him permission to get involved in our lives and in the lives of the people we are praying for. He can tell the great accuser of His character, "I am not interfering. They have asked for My help." As we ask for what we need and want, we grow in understanding of Him. God always answers prayer. Sometimes He quickly answers yes or no. More often He answers, "Wait. Watch. Don't fret. See what I will do for you." That answer often seems like indifference. "See? God doesn't care. My loved ones suffer, and He does nothing."

But in the midst of the waiting, He is teaching us to trust. Wait and listen. One key to patience is to keep busy with what you can do. Love those around you. Care for your fellow sufferers. Caring can be as simple as looking someone in the eyes and smiling. It can be as profound as whispering a prayer. Often we were worried about money. I gave up asking God to solve this problem or that. While His answers to problems seemed slow, the answer usually was, "Look at that! I made it go away."

We learned that He was working for us and solving our problems. My constant prayer became, "Help me listen for Your voice. Help me to obey that voice." We have become so close, that sometimes I just tell Him what I want.

One summer day during one of Jerry's hospital stays, I felt particularly harried. As I leapt into the car to go to the hospital, I prayed, "Lord, I wish my yard looked as if someone lived here." Later that day I came home to a manicured lawn. The church had seamlessly moved in to meet my needs. They did more than mow my lawn. They gave me courage. And God had a plan in place to take care of the desires of my heart even before I asked.

Since suffering is the price of freedom, why do we work to alleviate it? All of us who profess to follow Christ are walking pictures of Him. God uses us to tell others, "You are important to Me. I care that you hurt."

Chapter 6

Marriage is such a blessing. Of course, every time I say that, I wince in sympathy for my single friends or any divorced persons who have tried to stick it out when their spouse is not interested in working on their marriage. So many things work against marriage, but when two people are committed to each other and God, blessings abound.

Married couples face a host of challenges. First, our culture is more sexually explicit than ever. When I dated as a teen, promiscuity meant sexual activity before and apart from the marriage relationship. Now it means having a sexual relationship with more than one partner in the same time frame. Single again, I've dated men who are far from creeps and still believe it is okay to have sex within a few weeks of meeting as long as the relationship is exclusive. The mentality is that it's okay, even if it only lasts a few months. Being engaged no longer indicates that marriage is on the horizon. It usual indicates that the couple is sharing a household.

Next, divorce is becoming more acceptable. There are the hidden traps to make marriage a curse. Substance abuse makes so many people unfit for marriage and parenting. Sexual perversion destroys a lot of families. Credit cards encourage us to live beyond our means, and the mounting debt equals mounting stress. Sin hurts.

When we conceived Kelly, Jerry and I became more determined to stick it out. It is difficult to raise children. With societal values crumbling, a solid family becomes both more important and more difficult to find. Kelly was a relatively easy child to raise, but we still needed grandparents and a church full of people to do it well. I recently learned that children in a home where the male head of household is not their biological father are in greater danger of abuse of all kinds. Life is not only simpler when you all have the same last name, it is much safer for the children. Of course, I don't mean that all stepdads are creeps, but factor in our sexual climate and substance abuse and you see the potential for harm.

I try to remember that God is both Father to the fatherless and Husband to the widow. I picture Him holding me as He would a little girl, comforting me and reassuring me. I focus on all that He does to provide for my needs, including guiding my very thoughts. I rely heavily on a few friends who realize that it is no big deal if I cry. People who fuss over me when I am upset are a threat to me because of the depression. I must always guard against self-pity. My best friends comfort in a mater-of-fact way and encourage me to grow. I think we all do well to stretch, to force ourselves to do just a little bit more than we are comfortable with. I know if I didn't, I would curl up in bed and never leave it.

Jerry and I had many rough patches. We had to learn to avoid starting fights and bringing out the worst in each other. Marriage can be such a blessing when each wants to bring out the best in the other. We didn't alienate our friends from each other by broadcasting our faults in inflammatory language. My parents approved of Jerry. His family adored me. None of our friends and family grew to hate either of us because the other was whining about what a loser he had married. If respect for Jerry didn't constrain me, self-respect usually did. If your mate is really such a dud, what does it say about you? Another factor in highlighting each other's faults is what the children learn. They need to respect both parents. If you teach your children to disrespect your mate, it blows up in your face. It can lead to disrespect for all authority and an all expense paid vacation behind bars.

I wasted a lot of time thinking that Jerry was lazy. I didn't realize until he had the heart surgery that his health was so poor. He never complained. I rarely heard him say he hadn't slept well or that he ached from head to toe. Since he didn't complain, I forgot. That was a blessing when he got really sick since there wasn't much I could do to help. In the meantime, it was a curse. I thought he forgot his household chores because I wasn't important to him. Several times he lost his temper to the point of punching holes in walls and doors. The last time he did it, a school teacher told me that it was hostility directed toward the family. It didn't sound right. Three tantrums in ten years do not make an abuser. As I headed toward my breakdown, I realized that exhaustion can cause you to do crazy things. Many terrible fights can be avoided by a well-timed nap. Toddlers aren't the only ones who get cranky and destructive.

Oddly enough, it was my breakdown that made me see how much Jerry loved me. His offer to do whatever it took to make me happy was genuine. I was accustomed to taking care of myself and helping every-one else. I didn't know how to ask for help. He didn't suddenly become Super Mom able to vacuum whole rooms in a single bound, but he ten-derly encouraged me to rest. He held me when I cried, and he listened to my fears. Three weeks before he passed, I shared some thoughtless remark that had terrified me for several years. The comment was so per-sonal that I couldn't share it with anyone else. I was so frightened I could hardly choke out the words. His comfort brought the ridiculous statement into perspective. He helped to provide an environment congenial to my healing. Although Jerry's sickness ended in death, I did everything in my power to improve the quality of his life.

Nowadays you must be determined to stay together and do what-ever it takes to make your marriage happy. Bad patches should be just that—bad patches and not whole fields awaiting a harvest of bitterness. Bad patches are warnings to pull together. Have fun together as a cou-ple and as a family. Some people have to schedule this. Focus on what is good about each other even when facing the things that need work. Don't pretend your marriage is perfect. You wouldn't ignore a crack in the base-ment wall and expect it to go away nor would you attack it spontaneously with a sledgehammer.

Prayer changes lives. Jerry and I used to get in terrible arguments when Kelly was little. We had lived our own lives for far longer than we had been a family, so we had to learn how to get along as one unit instead of two.

I took to leaving the room and praying for peace in our family. Often one of us would fall asleep. Didn't I tell you we are just cranky toddlers?

Our marriage is proof that anyone can have a happy marriage. God wants this for all married people, and He will do whatever it takes to help us create strong households. Our biggest input is being willing for this to happen.

Chapter 7

I have been a devout Seventh-day Adventist for more than half of my life. When I lose sight of Christ, it seems like a complicated game of not offending the brethren. As our pastor said recently, "Sometimes the sheep have teeth." Little woolies aren't always as cute as the ones on Easter cards.

On a serious note, the church, all who accept that God has done everything necessary to give us eternal life, is His bride. Whether or not we have membership in a local congregation, we reflect on His character because we claim to follow Him. I know beautiful Christians who do not engage in corporate worship. To remain faithful and strong alone is a more difficult path, and I do not encourage it. However, some are too badly hurt by the politics of church. (Politics occur wherever you have a group of people trying to work together to accomplish something. It isn't always a bad thing.) I sympathize with those who worship at home because I have scars from where my stupidity has collided with the church. I understand because my intolerance and anger have given scars that I can never heal. Church membership is not for the faint hearted. I thank God for the pastor who baptized me. He hammered home this vital message: "Look to Christ as your example. Your brothers and sisters will discourage you sooner or later. Look to Christ as your example. Always look to Christ as your example."

Christ will always be there for you. Your brothers and sisters are as finite as you are. They will forget to call and be timid about visiting. Their own ill health or discouragement will keep them from encouraging you when you really need it. Christ is always there. Help them to help you. Thank them when they say the right thing. Thank them for caring about you when they rub you the wrong way in an effort to help. Be quick to assume that they mean well. Carefully teach them a better way if it is really important. There is something about living with a dying man. You quit fussing over the incidentals.

It used to disturb me that only the pastor visited Jerry regularly. Although he hadn't been an active member of the church for years, he still had friends there. Where were they? I suspect that the ones our age had trouble dealing with it. It's not nice to face your own mortality while the kids are still in high school. John, an elder who truly cares about others, made me realize how difficult this is. At the calling hours, he shook my hand, gazed into my eyes, and gushed over how well I was holding up. He then practically ran from the casket. He greeted everyone in the room while carefully keeping his back to the casket. Jerry was only four years older than John. As my load of grief lifted, I was able to see what others were bearing at the time. We can't always see the big picture, but we do well to assume folks do their best.

Jerry was grateful for what he got. I was so sad and discouraged his last Christmas because it appeared that no one was going to visit him. Then on Christmas Eve quite a few showed up, which cheered me up.

Another feeling I struggled with was one of frustration that no one was able or willing to help me care for Jerry. One day he told me that he didn't mind that no one came. I realized that I was all the church members Jerry needed. His acceptance freed me from bitterness. I must add that the church prayed and prayed for us—seven Sabbaths in a row during morning prayer. When someone says they pray for you, never reject it as an empty gesture. Often it doesn't seem like much, but in reality it is the finest gift we can give one another.

I empathize with pastors. I think every one of them, male and female, should be given a blue suit with a bull's eye on the back. The harder they work to create an environment in which we can grow in Christ, the more tattered the bull's eye will be. Anyone who works tirelessly to teach others about God incurs the wrath of Satan. We who are spiritual should not join his efforts.

As far as I am concerned, the only difference between a pastor and a lay member is the degree of responsibility. I think we all would do well to make the standards of the pastor or elder our goals in character development. Honesty, integrity, confidentiality, and the ability to hide our shock are all valuable in helping others to see what God is like. The character of God and His right to rule over us is what it is all about. The failings of a pastor are more irritating simply because their role is more visible. Their responsibilities are greater because more look to them as an example. A small flaw in a pastor can be interpreted as an excuse for open sin in a younger or weaker Christian.

Pastors are like us. They come in all different shapes and sizes and have a variety of gifts. They do not have all the gifts, nor do they all have identical gifts. Their primary job is to teach us how to share God with others. Some think a pastor is negligent if he doesn't do everything in the church. I think his job is to make sure the important stuff gets done. Who does it is immaterial. How well it is done can be immaterial since you have to start somewhere before you can get good at a task.

This spring I embroidered a tapestry for the church. There were five pictures of Christ, scenes from New Testament stories. I looked forward to making it because I always feel close to God when I have an embroidery hoop in my hand. The work did not go well at first. Sometimes

I can be so insecure. I was sure that this one or that one in the church would disapprove of particular choices I had made. My biggest worry was the skin color. I went to a hobby shop where they have a great variety of embroidery floss. Not one color closely resembled any known skin tone. Black people aren't anymore black than I am white. None of the browns looked quite right either. I used a shade I had at home—a dark khaki that blended in perfectly with the cloth. It stood out just well enough to be seen. Although Christ was Semitic when born as a man, His race is immaterial. He was one of us; however, I fretted about offending my brothers and sisters.

I didn't do much embroidery the first week because the task was so unpleasant. Sunday Christ rapped me on the head as I struggled with cloth and thread. "It's about Me. The whole point of this project is to glorify Me. Don't worry about what others think because this is between us." Of course! So much prayer had already gone into the project. For almost three months I worked on the canvass as if I were playing at His feet.

That tapestry is like the church, each stitch an individual member. No two stitches were exactly alike and yet the great variety of shapes and colors are necessary to make the whole picture and to make it well. Many of the stitches are flawed, and yet their flaws will go unnoticed in the majesty of Christ.

In one picture Christ was standing in a boat about to calm the seas. The rigging was bare because of the storm. "Show me how to make the rigging," I prayed while working on another picture. While stopping to look through an embroidery book, one of the same old illustrations I had looked at before and hadn't struck me popped off the page. "This is it!" I boldly used my new stitch. I executed it inaccurately, but it still did the job well. Anything placed in His hands becomes beautiful.

We need to be so careful when we judge one another. I could say that we aren't supposed to, but let's deal with reality. The church body is sometimes called to judge an individual because we are responsible for one another. Which one of us would allow our children to routinely place their hands on a hot burner? Yet the church often turns a blind eye when we turn away from Christ. This is far more dangerous. On a lighter note, we are human and prone to judging. Either way we must be careful not to judge according to motive. Remember our buddy Job? Satan accused him on his motives. "Job serves You because he has it easy." Look what Job went through to prove Satan wrong? Motives can't be proven in the short term. Assigning inaccurate motives can do untold harm.

Motives are important in studying out how to avoid sin and temptation to sin. We need to figure out why we do what we do. A friend who will gently and carefully question our motive can do much to protect us from sin. However, when we start beating one another up according to motives, we can't learn anything.

When our faults, large or small, become known to the church, they should be dealt with as quietly as possible. If one dresses inappropriately for church, speak to that person privately or ignore it. If you don't know him well enough to tactfully suggest that he is a distraction from worship, then you don't know him well enough to broadcast his error in judgment. What might be quickly and quietly fixed with a few hand-me-downs may become an incident that drives the individual from church if not handled appropriately.

It is important to deal with a situation when we feel offended. "You hurt my feelings!" may not be the best way to broach the subject. A calm, pleasant demeanor encourages open, honest communication. We all think better when we don't feel attacked. Last week I felt deeply offended that my donation to a disaster relief project still sat neglected in the hallway. I was too tired to deal with it civilly, so I asked Christ to deal with it. This week I had the opportunity to mention it to the woman in charge of community service. "Oh Linda! Where is it? I will make sure it is delivered." She had not tried to snub me. The bundle had been mislaid. Think of how much time and energy I could have wasted brooding if I hadn't bothered talking to her. Think of the trouble I could have caused if I had whispered all around about her. Satan likes that. It makes the church inefficient in telling others about God, and it paints a picture contrary to all we say about Him and His love.

Chapter 8

We didn't bury Jerry's ashes until the third of June. At first the pastor was concerned over my postponing the burial. An extra week didn't seem bad to him when I explained my rationale. "In all of this I considered the needs of everyone." In the air my hand drew a wide circle between us. "Jerry will be buried with military honors. This is for me. I want to soak up every aspect of the ceremony."

"Good. Good," he simply said.

The burial was at 2 p.m. Somehow Kelly and I arrived fashionably late. She had trouble getting ready, and I wasn't about to push her. I limited attendance to family and David, the one friend who would come at three in the morning if we needed him. The pastor greeted me in the hallway of the funeral home. He shook my hand and said, "It is an honor to serve."

Taking up the role of widow, I spoke. "It is an honor you earned." The only time he didn't visit Jerry in the hospital was when he was on vacation. Every day for three weeks, two weeks, or whatever it took. Sometimes he would go in the middle of the night because he knew Jerry didn't sleep soundly. He stood as a faithful soldier guarding Jerry's heart.

Without fanfare we followed a funeral home vehicle to the nearby cemetery. His ashes were in a wooden box carved in China. It reminded me of his Japanese puzzle box. Things had gone full circle so quickly. Kevin had slipped us some cash on the day he died. We used some of it to purchase the box. To our delight we got it on clearance and asked that the tag be kept inside with the ashes. I picture Jerry on resurrection morning as we meet each other in the air showing me the tag. He will then scold me. "I told you a Hefty bag would do." We viewed death so irreverently.

It was cold and rainy for June. I took comfort in my gray wool coat. I squared my shoulders as I took my seat beside the open grave. Pride swelled within me when a veteran presented me with the flag. Jerry had never considered himself much of a soldier. He always deferred to those who had seen combat in Vietnam, but nonetheless he had served. I was proud to live in a country that cared for Jerry in his illness. The government fed and clothed us when he could no longer work. The government instituted the unemployment insurance that allowed me to care for him between jobs. The government would continue to care for Kelly since her father could not. I could picture us begging in Calcutta where poverty and illness are not relieved because they are bitter gifts from gods who do not care.

Jerry had not served his country with distinction. He had been an army photographer who had quietly recorded medical procedures. His documentation helped advance medical science, but the immediate results of his work had been negligible. The most exciting event in his military career was when he passed out filming a surgery. He always looked slyly proud when he got to the part about all the nurses fussing over him.

Although he died at home, he went bravely into the night. He suffered much and yet didn't cease to be a husband and father. A couple of weeks before he died, Kelly had come home for some dental appointments. Although I would growl at her to get some sleep, she always had her 2 a.m. visit with Daddy. He taught her so much in those fifteen years—everything from how to shampoo her own hair like a big girl to understanding Mommy to accepting others as they are. I told her about Christ. He showed her His character. Jerry glorified God in his illness. There is no greater honor than to praise God when life is black.

We were warned that the 21-gun salute would be loud. The first crack ripped open the sky, and I flinched. All three rounds expressed the magnitude of my loss. Together Jerry and I had functioned as one whole, well person. Afterwards, they gathered the shell casings and presented them to me. The silk bag transformed into a treasure. The ten-year-old inside me laughed. Widowhood would not crush me. What we had gone through had molded Kelly and I into soldiers. In Christ we would find everything we needed to march forward.

Recently I read an article on courage. Written by a U.S. senator it dared to suggest that the word bravery and courage are tossed around too lightly. He felt that these words should be limited to heroic acts in combat. He pooh-poohed the notion that honesty in the face of serious consequences, compassion where it isn't popular, and following one's convictions in the face of opposition could be bravery. How does one develop the character to risk life and limb for others? Courage is a muscle built up by smaller acts of courage.

Jerry had exemplified these smaller acts of courage. As a teen he joined a church different from that of his family. In an effort to guard himself from temptation, he attended a Christian high school. He endured the stigma of being a charity case for the opportunity of learning more about Jesus. He walked two miles each way to school through bad neighborhoods. A classmate was badly beaten making the same trek. We joked that the trip to school was uphill both ways.

He had the courage to place others first. Money was tight for us. One day a neighbor came to borrow money for much needed baby supplies. With his blessing, I gave away our grocery money. We knew we would never see it again, but the baby was more important. Another time we were worshipping in a small rural church. Some men stopped to ask for gas money. The pastor had not yet arrived, and the church members handled it by not handling it. Outside the church, Jerry was talking to the men who not only were out of gas but were also lost. He came to me and told me about their situation. After talking it over, Jerry went with them to charge some gasoline. I teased them about not forgetting to bring Jerry back. Suddenly the elders huddled in fervent prayer for Jerry, and two women behind me carried on about how dangerous and foolish he was. Jerry was given a hero's welcome by the frightened congregation when he returned. Jerry never had the opportunity to lay down his life for another. However, where would we be if we hoarded our courage for such times?

When I left the graveside, the pastor looked me square in the eyes and quoted Don Moen's song lyrics, "God will make a way when there seems to be no way. He works in ways we cannot see. He will make a way for me." I drank it up like a cup of courage for the days ahead. God would make a way. It lay in the footsteps of courage Jerry had forged. Little steps, little acts of courage that Kelly and I could follow on our way to glory.

Part 2

Hope for the Hurting

Chapter 9

Each chapter in this section is a block in the patchwork of what makes us well. Some of the pieces may not make sense until you see the whole. Please don't give up on this section. Read it all. Feel free to tailor what has worked for me into a comforter that  suits your needs and tastes. This section of the book is my comforter, my pattern of values and coping skills. I pray that it inspires you to take an active role in seeking good mental health.

I do stress the importance of medications and professional help. If your mind is not running on all fours, the greatest advice in the world won't help. When I finally sought the help of a psychiatrist, friends and therapists had already taught me many healthy coping skills. The drugs made the difference between textbook knowledge and practical application.

I remember as a child that I was coached and coached on how to swing a baseball bat. Although I understood the directions, it was a while before the bat and the ball connected. Much practice occurred between understanding and accomplishment. Throughout life I understood so much about how to live well, how to think constructively. I could even do it to some extent. The medication allowed me to think clearly and to do what I already understood.

If possible we should seek help while we are young. Teens often are helped by talk therapy alone. Untreated depression causes peculiar coping strategies that may be difficult to unlearn when depression is under control. Untreated depression can lead to self-medication with alcohol and illegal, addictive drugs. These habits can seriously hinder progress toward a happy, productive life.

I am personally cautious about herbal remedies and nutritional supplements. I use some for pain management and overall health. A diet low in fat featuring fruits, vegetables, and whole grains coupled with moderate exercise does wonders for the disposition without conflicting with medications. If you are on prescriptions, make sure you consult with your doctor or pharmacist about specific herbal remedies. Keep your family aware of any changes in your regimen. When depression is out of control, judgment is impaired. Once judgment is impaired it can be a short, treacherous slide to despair and suicide.

God, professional care, and supportive family and friends are important to the comforter we make of our lives. Training or disciplining your mind not to dwell on negative thoughts is also valuable. Medication will only do so much. Disciplining your mind can make the difference between being functional and really enjoying life.

The Bible is the sturdy thread that holds my comforter together. I will paraphrase passages in my own words for ease of reading. I will provide references for those who want to read it in context. I highly recommend doing that.

Keep this in mind: You can't have a very good comforter without all the pieces. God can fill in the gaps while you collect the bits and fobs and stitch away, but it takes years to get it together. Enjoy the process. It is called growing up. As long as you draw breath, you are not too old to start.

A secondary purpose of this section of the book is to help your loved ones understand what you are going through and what might be helpful to you. While understanding our experience is important, constant coddling is crippling. Like everyone else on this planet, we need to keep growing in order to stay healthy.

Our lives can become fluffy, durable comforters benefiting others as well as ourselves. God is eager to help us become happy and useful. Even in our darkest moments, He is working for our good.

Chapter 10

No one pays attention to the back of a comforter, and yet it is so important. Years ago I made one for my husband. I used pre-quilted nylon fabric. It was a real bargain but not good for comforters. Right now it lies behind my bed because it slides right off the other covers. The comforter helps no one because of the backing.

God is our backing whether we acknowledge Him or not. There is no life apart from Him. In Him we live and move and have our being (Acts 17:28). Recognizing this fact is an important key to enjoying life.

God loves us no matter what. He is not an ogre raining misery on our heads. He forgives the blackest deeds. He loves the inhabitants of death row as much as He loves the most shining examples of humanity. He weeps over each one who refuses to have anything to do with Him (Matthew 23:37).

Bad things happen because of sin in the world. Sin is a separation from God that shows itself in bad deeds. Adam and Eve started it on this planet when they ate from the tree (Genesis 3). I don't believe the tree had magical properties. Choosing to disobey God revealed a lack of trust in Him.

All sinful acts boil down to a lack of trust. We steal because we don't trust God to provide. We lie because we don't trust Him to help us face the truth. We covet another's mate or stuff because we don't allow God to help us enjoy what is ours. Lying is the most dangerous sin. God can't help us fix what's broken when we firmly declare that everything is fine.

When sin causes us to suffer, God is not punishing us. When it is the result of our own poor choices, it is the natural consequences of our acts. When a child habitually forgets his homework, should mom make an extra trip to school every morning? Once she has helped her child organize, not covering for him may be the most important lesson of all. If we don't take responsibility for our lives, God may very well allow us to experience the consequences.

Other suffering is the result of living on a planet where sin has reigned for thousands of years. Why does God allow it? His most precious gift to all of us is free will. He does not want us to follow Him because we are afraid and feel we have no choice. Sin originated in heaven (Isaiah 14:12–15). In order for all of God's creation to serve and love Him in freedom, sin must run its course on earth. Just before we are ready to destroy ourselves, He will return and put sin to an end forever. He will take with Him the living and the dead who have chosen to trust Him. With great sorrow He will leave behind those who want nothing to do with Him.

Jesus Christ is the perfect blending of humanity and divinity (John 1:1, 14). Satan demands that we pay for our sins. We are very sinful. If everyone who ever lived died horribly and miserably, we still would not have paid for our crimes. Only Jesus could do that when He died on the cross. He paid for absolutely everyone. Each person has a free ticket to heaven and eternal life with God. Although it is absolutely free to us, it has cost God more than we can imagine. If we toss the ticket aside or stuff it deep into a pocket, it is no less valid, no less paid for, than if we use it. If we refuse to use the ticket, we ultimately are not with God. There is no life apart from God.

What does this mean to us here and now? God loves us. God wants us healthy and happy. There is no everlasting hell to shun. There is a glorious universe to explore when He returns. God does not want bad things for us. God does not delight in our sufferings.

God promises not to put upon us more than we can bear (1 Corinthians 10:13), but in the midst of the chaos that was my life for a number of years, I questioned that promise.

In August of 1998 my father died. I had difficulty mourning this loss. My husband's father died two weeks later. We were stunned because he had been on death's doorstep the whole eleven years Jerry and I had been married. Then other friends died or moved away, narrowing my circle of support.

In April of 1999 my mother had a stroke. Although she wasn't demanding, for a few months she required lots of help. Friends criticized me for neglecting Jerry and Kelly. I was hurt and angry. No one was volunteering to shoulder part of my load, but they sure had advice on dumping Mom. Family is a tight bond formed for the protection and growth of its members. Even Kelly understood that a family works together and sometimes one member needs more help than the others. Because of the death of my father, I had trouble trusting God. Now I guarded my appearance. I carefully hid the fact that I was falling apart because I couldn't risk anymore criticism.

Does this sound like plenty enough? It got worse. I became less and less able to sleep. I stopped taking the antidepressant prescribed by the family doctor because it was no longer effective. I decided to tough it out without any drugs. Life got so black that suicide looked like the only effective painkiller. Do you feel that way? Do you have a plan for taking your life? If you do, get help now. You are priceless to God. He can heal you and restore you. Get help now! Clinical depression has an 80 percent cure rate.

In mid-November I ended up in a psychiatrist's office. I was terrified. Antidepressants work differently in each person, and the side effects vary from person to person. I was afraid of becoming a zombie from the wrong meds. Of course, I am happy to say that the risk is worth the long-term gain. Be honest with the doctor. Pray for the professionals who care for you. God wants you healthy and happy. He will bless their work if you ask.

Wasn't all of this more than I could bear? I crashed. I landed face in the dirt with a bloody nose and grit in my teeth. How bad can it get? I wondered.

The day I called the doctor's office, I admitted I couldn't do it alone. It was then that God sent constant reminders of His love. People faithfully prayed for me.

Antidepressants often take a month to be effective. With most of them you build up to the recommended dosage. It took several months for the drugs to help because I was stubborn about taking the full dosage. It took a couple of years to get well and strong because I had fifteen months of insomnia to recover from and more troubles ahead.

More? Hadn't I already cracked under the load God allowed me? Ironically, the breakdown was actually the way of escape God promises when you are sorely tried.

In July of 2000 Jerry had open-heart surgery. It was a miracle he lived long enough to be diagnosed. A heart attack before surgery would have been fatal. As it was, he was under the knife for six hours and had five bypasses if I remember correctly. I was terrified. This was a horror movie someone had forgotten to film. The prognosis included being home in six days and back to work in six months. The reality was in the hospital for one month and permanent disability.

Now surely this was too much! No. Our marriage had been on rocky ground. Through all of this terror, God was giving us a chance to regroup and rebuild. All of Jerry's energy had been needed to hold down a job and support us. Now he could focus on being a husband and father. Now he could sleep while I worked and the three of us could have more time to pay attention to one another.

God will make every effort to guide us into His kingdom and make us fit for eternal life in a sinless universe. All Jerry's trials helped him to trust God to meet his needs. All our trials increased our faith, or trust, in God. Now my telling about those trials is helping others. The pain is really worth it.

Recently I told Kelly, "Look at the doors God is opening for us. When we meet up with Daddy, he will be so proud." Jerry always underestimated his importance in my life. He felt that he held me back. I picture him grinning shyly and saying, "See? The best thing I did for you was die." He will then laugh boldly because he will fully understand how much he is loved.

God must be the backing of our comforter. He never leaves you cold and lonely. He always love, forgives, and guides. He is love itself (1 Corinthians 13; 1 John 4:8).

Chapter 11

People are the fluffy middle that makes our comforter warm and snuggly. No man is an island. While solitude can be beneficial and independence a good thing, not one of us stands alone. We are meant to form one body under the authority of Christ (1 Corinthians 12). However, because I have clinical depression, there are times when I am very careful with whom I spend my time.

We are made in the image of God. We are destined to be like Jesus and to live with Him forever (Colossians 3:9, 10). Only our free will can separate us from our destiny. Once we choose to follow Him, He will not let us go easily. He will move heaven and earth to keep us safely in His arms.

We each have a right to whatever makes us healthy and strong. As some like to phrase it, we should boldly pursue whatever it takes to remain aware of God's presence in our lives. Friends who cause us to doubt our worth or ability to improve are not a fluffy middle. They are abrasive; they chafe the spots that need healing. Folks who encourage damaging behaviors such as substance abuse and sexual addictions offer a blowtorch that can destroy your connection to a healthy network of friends.

Who do we want to fill our comforter? Do we want a collection of "yes" men? "You can do it, Linda! Go for it! Jump off the high dive." This sounds good until you learn that I can barely swim. Without some serious training, I have no business jumping off the diving board into the deep end. We all can benefit from cheerleaders, but we need more than that. Christ's body is made up of a variety of parts for a reason. They are all important.

We also need people to remind us of reality. They keep us from jumping out of planes without parachutes. They help us discover and hone our gifts. They know we are beautiful in Christ. They see the diamond in the dirt. They do not blindly encourage our wildest assumptions nor do they hand us rose-colored glasses.

Blue skies and green grass look best through clear lenses. Rose-colored glasses are fun now and then; however, if we wore them all the time, we might not notice the grass turning brown. We might miss God calling softly to water the lawn. Once the grass is dead, the rose-colored glasses won't fix it.

Above all, we need people who trust God to help us figure it out. On the one hand, they are not visibly shocked or upset with our setbacks. On the other hand, they set clear boundaries so we don't drive them away. When I was severely depressed, I had the emotional maturity of a ten-year-old. Children that age don't pick up on hints. Direct commands and plain instructions help them to function well in society. What God helps us figure out is our own individual paths to getting back to the point where once again we remember the needs of others on our own.

When depression is severe, I don't recommend heavily confiding in friends of the opposite sex. Above all, don't complain about your mate to those friends. When depression is severe, it is very easy to lean on friends too hard. Strong bonds of sympathy can lead to adultery. Depression wrecks enough relationships. Don't throw yourself in the path of an affair. Even if nothing happens, it can destroy your reputation. Don't underestimate the value of a good reputation. You may not care about it today, but when you end up living it down for decades, you will care.

With all that said, the most helpful friend I had after the breakdown was a man who walked into my life two years later. Bud had training as a counselor, and we were agreed on the need to be careful, the need to follow the rules to avoid my leaning on him too hard. The primary rule was that we always spoke out in the open where there would be no question of our reputations. In hindsight it would have been helpful if his wife were more involved.

When I started to confide in him, my mind was a tangled jungle of wild thoughts and unrealistic expectations. I tend to be paranoid. Unfortunately, my paranoia was fueled by one or two who wanted to hurt me. Often I was overwhelmed by what I call endless loops of garbage. Your mind clutches tightly one useless negative thought. It expresses itself in a sentence or two and those words replay forever. "How could they treat me like that?" Although the loops were often true, dwelling on them helped no one. The circular thinking just distracted me from God.

Bud untangled my thoughts. He never tolerated any rudeness that might eventually drive him away. He directed my mind to God while painstakingly correcting the inaccuracies in my perceptions. If he found it tedious, he never let on. He had the courage to agree with me where my perceptions were right. This flat out destroyed some of the endless loops. Once the thought had been heard and understood by someone I respected, I could let go of it.

He didn't lecture me to wholesale abandon my negative thoughts. There were real wounds that needed to be cleansed by my tears so that they wouldn't be infected by bitterness. Forcing me to hide these memories deep inside would have only made a worse mess later. Cleanse your sorrows with tears as often as necessary. Eventually you will learn how to shift swiftly from cleansing tears back to thoughts that give you joy.

As Bud straightened and guided my thoughts, I watched him work. Eventually I pitched in because I knew what to do. Now, in God's strength, I can banish the endless loops. In His strength, I am able to find sanity and peace, to focus on the pure, the true, and the lovely (Philippians 4:8). Remember that just because it is true doesn't mean it is worth dwelling on for hours.

Chapter 12

I once had a pretty comforter fall apart for lack of good thread. I had spent hours at the sewing machine, and my work was coming apart. I spent as much time mending it, and it still had holes. Strong thread would have made my work last for years and years.

The thread of our comforters should be the Bible because God speaks to us through it. It is the first and last word on wisdom, grace, and beauty. It chronicles the events of real people with messy problems. God's work in their lives shows what He wants to do for us. Do you wonder if you are too dirty for God? Moses, who led God's people to the Promised Land, committed murder as a young man (Exodus 2; 6). Rahab, a harlot in Jericho, is mentioned in the genealogy of Christ (Matthew 1:5). King David, a man after God's own heart, had more wives than any man needs. Still, he stole Bathsheba from Uriah the Hittite (2 Samuel 11:2–10).

If God could clean up these folks and fit them for heaven, He can do wonders for us. The fact that I am alive and writing this is a great testimony to His loving eagerness to heal and restore His children.

It is not enough to know about the Bible or to listen to good preaching. Although I am blessed greatly by Christian radio, it is not a substitute for a few quiet minutes reading the Bible for myself. God inhabits His word (John 1:1), so we need to go there and dig in.

Does Scripture seem like gibberish to you? Don't give up. Modern translations do much to make Scripture understandable. My personal favorite is the New International Version. The Contemporary English Version is also good if you aren't much of a reader. Both are translations. This becomes important when you need to know exactly what God says. Paraphrase Bibles are not as precise as translations. A paraphrase edition will take liberties with the original language in order to make the passage more applicable to our culture.

There are also tools to help you understand the Bible. A concordance is a large book listing the key words of the Bible in alphabetical order. Let's say you can't remember where to find the story of the woman at the well. Look up woman. Of course, there are lots of verses with that word. The story is in the Gospels—Matthew, Mark, Luke, and John. Just look at the references in those books. And bingo! You found it.

A topical Bible works a little like an encyclopedia. You look up a subject, and it lists all the verses on that topic. Some of them will be written out and others will be listed so that you can look them up for yourself. It is a little smaller than a concordance.

A Bible encyclopedia explains things about the culture and language used in the time the Bible was written. For example, you can look up the word wedding and learn more about the customs of the time. This will help you get more meaning out of the parable of the wedding feast.

Bible commentaries are another source for understanding the Bible. They come in a variety of sizes. You can get one the size of a set of encyclopedias that covers the entire Bible. You can also find smaller ones dealing with a particular book of the Bible. These books offer a more comprehensive body of information than the encyclopedia and yet similar in nature. It will go over the Bible verse by verse, explaining the original language and customs that will give greater insight into the passage.

If you bought all of these volumes, that would be a lot of books. Fortunately, you can find software for your computer or Internet sites that contain the same information. BibleGateway.com has been my religious library for years. It is easy to search the Bible for keywords and read in countless translations, all with the click of the mouse. And it's free!

Depression can turn a brilliant mind into mush. Don't let it detour you from Bible reading. Don't be discouraged that you can't think clearly. It will not last forever. God inhabits His word. Read even if you don't understand. God's presence will give you a peace and calmness that no one can take from you. Read. Keep reading. God will guide you into understanding at the proper time. He knows what is best for you. He will reveal Himself more and more as He heals your minds.

When my depression was at an all time low, I decided to read the Bible through. This was when I had my breakdown. For no logical reason, I started in the book of Jeremiah. On the surface this is a dismal book. God's people have hit rock bottom in personal impurity and national unfaithfulness. He was ready to cart them off to Babylon. Repeatedly they faced the consequences of their sins without repenting. God had to do something drastic. This was worse than habitually forgetting your homework.

Daddy God had a right to be angry. The best of human fathers would have snapped by now, spewing verbal abuse. Not Daddy God. He encouraged His people to turn back to Him. He promised to give them hope and a future (Jeremiah 29:11, 12). He desired the joy of their company even in distant Babylon.

Just prior to my breakdown, I was far from God. I was Israel. God had guided me to the book that would help me most. I did not understand every detail of the book, but it shouted, "There is hope. You will get better. Just hang on tight to Me."

Scripture is the sturdy thread for our comforters. Nothing we stitch together with a "thus says the Lord" will fall apart. Now that we have the right thread we are ready to sort through the blocks.

Chapter 13

Now we start the fun part of our comforter. This is the part everyone sees. A good comforter has a variety of blocks. The greater the variety of textures, shades, and patterns, the better the comforter is.

Emotions are the texture of life. They cannot be denied. To try to live without feeling is to deny an important part of how God makes us. The more we bottle up unpleasant emotions the less room we have for joy, happiness, and delight. Whenever we try to deny our feelings or repress them long term, they will pop out in very inappropriate ways later.

I experienced that when Jerry died. The first few weeks I coasted on relief that Jerry wasn't suffering. Then I became so rude to people—cashiers, clerks, bank tellers. It disturbed me because I know firsthand how hard it can be to wait on the public. I was becoming a monster. God had carried us so well during Jerry's illness that I couldn't admit that I was angry with Him. It made no sense. It seemed supremely unfair, and I didn't want to go there.

Guess what? Mankind is sinful. Unfairness comes to us as naturally as breathing. I was angry with God because losing Jerry still hurt terribly. Not even losing my father hurt like this. I naively thought that God would shield me from this pain. Of course not! I needed to experience this loss completely so that I could better help others who are hurting. None of us have a right to expect to have an easier life simply because we know God.

At one point, I read that anger is an immature expression of sorrow or grief. I've been angry most of my life. I've discovered over the years that crying on God's shoulder when it hurts eliminates a good deal of that anger and frees me up to enjoy what is good and happy. However, some of us are angry because we weren't taught how to properly express anger. Other times, when we experience many losses in a relatively short period of time, anger is a healthy coping mechanism. It keeps us from curling up in bed and neglecting the needs of those who depend upon us.

Now God has given me some useful tools for handling anger. Ideally, anger should be dealt with immediately so that it doesn't grow into an unruly monster. First, try not to yell. I find a low, deep voice to be effective without creating a scene. Never publicly embarrass someone who makes you angry. The purpose of anger is to clear your mind and rectify a situation. Control prevents the situation from becoming worse. Next, try to be fair in your anger. Don't exaggerate the problem. Try to assume the person means well and has valid reasons for their behavior. Lastly, don't dredge up every past mistake. Stick to the point you are trying to make. Dealing with someone's anger is unpleasant even when it is handled well. If you follow these tips, the other person will have an easier time listening to you instead of loading up for his turn to shotgun blast you back.

Sometimes if my anger is wild and unfair I will take it to God first. In His presence you don't have to be fair, nice, or even rational. Blow! Go ahead and blow up. Use whatever words pop into your head. God already knows your heart. You might as well let the venom spew forth in the safety of His presence. He will not spread the pain by gossiping about you. He will not retaliate because you have been cruel.

When you are spent, gently and carefully He will help you see the other side of it. Without humiliating you, He will show you where you have erred and where you are right. He will show you how to remedy the problem gracefully or by His grace. Look up grace in a concordance. It always belongs to God or comes from Him. It means unmerited favor—a kindness you didn't earn.

Some of us are prone to anger because we grew up in households where anger abounded and there were no healthy outlets for its expression. I do not condemn these families. Almost all of us do the best we can with what we have. However, there is a physiological difference in the brain of someone who has grown up in an atmosphere of constant arguing. The part of the brain that deals with anger is chronically irritated. We are physiologically more prone to blowing up. The more tired we are, the more likely it will happen. This is not to excuse bad behavior. This is just another reason to value proper sleep and healthy eating.

When anger is deep-rooted, counseling can be very helpful. It isn't always a simple matter of learning how to control it. Sometimes a ballistic temper is the results of years of suffering injustices as a child and being truly powerless to change anything for the better. Such wounds must be surrendered to God. While forgiving those who have wronged you is vital to your functioning well, healing may be imperfect on this earth.

Forgiving horrible, black sins that have been done to you is not an act of letting the guilty party off easy. It is vital to your wholeness and happiness. It does not come easy, but God will never give up on you. It is difficult to forgive someone who feels he has done no wrong. Still, you need to do this for yourself. You can't live and breathe on this planet without eventually hurting someone. Christ died for all of our sins, not just the more socially acceptable ones. He tells us we must forgive if we wish to receive forgiveness (Luke 11:4).

It's truly simple. You can't receive all the good things He has for you if your arms are full of garbage and you refuse to let go. As you let go of bad things, He fills your arms with peace, joy, and happiness. As you realize how much He forgives you, you become more skilled at forgiving others.

I have learned three things to help me avoid embarrassing temper fits. First, daily ask God to protect you from the temptation to sin, particularly in your anger. Next, accept the fact that you will be more likely to be upset, discouraged, or angry in the evening. When problems happen at night, remind yourself that a good night's sleep makes everything look better. An extra prayer here goes a long way. Finally, discipline yourself to give God every problem. Most of the times we don't need an immediate plan of action. God can hold onto it while we rest. When we are rested, He can show us how to deal with the problem gracefully. It's okay not to have all the answers. He does. Be patient with yourself.

Humor and cheerfulness are undervalued emotions. Humor eases tensions and frees our minds so that when we return to the problem at hand we have renewed vigor. When you are depressed, there is no end to seemingly insurmountable problems. Putting away your clothes and going through the junk mail are Herculean tasks. Give yourself permission to forget your troubles and laugh. When depression is deep, we might not laugh aloud. However, it is still helpful. As we heal, we will have trained ourselves to value humor. Cheerfulness is a delightful blend of hope and kindness. With God's help we can be cheerful all the time. Cheerfulness banishes fear and irritation. It is not loud or abrasive nor does it demand that others respond in kind. It is not dependent on circumstances. Cheerfulness is healing (Proverbs 17:22).

Happiness is highly overrated. We chase after it in our careers, our family life, and our shopping trips. The harder we trot after it, the quicker it flees.

Stand still. Just stand still. Remember God. Relentlessly pursue whatever it takes to sense His presence. Seek His will for your life. This is joy. It feels just like happiness only it is based on His enduring love for you and not on circumstances. As we learn to value joy, we will become happier because we are more likely to notice the things or circumstances that make us happy.

The Bible will help you to discern His will for your life. Freely ask for the wisdom to discern it and the courage to follow it. His will for your life is not an arbitrary assignment of tasks designed to make your life miserable. While trials may be used to get you there, His ultimate will is that you use the gifts He has already given you. These gifts are things you may enjoy more and more as you develop them. Writing is one of those gifts in my life. So has been waiting on tables and now caring for the disabled in their homes. For decades sewing, crocheting, and embroidery have been gifts I've used. In the last several years, I started making things for the needy. The church became aware of my mission that they asked me to start a small group ministry. There are about twelve of us now, and it is amazing what we are accomplishing. The work is worth our effort. It is both a joy and a delight that I would never have thought possible as I recovered from the breakdown. God uses our failings and our wounds. He makes the ugliest things steppingstones to glory.

Without the emotion of hope, we can't live for long. Hope gets us up in the morning and causes us to pursue our dreams. A lack of hope crushes our spirits. A prolonged lack of hope destroys us. Restoring the emotion of hope is as easy as opening your Bible and as difficult as choosing to believe. God wants you in His kingdom. God will do whatever it takes to fit you for His kingdom. All He needs is your permission. No matter how ugly and dirty you are, He can clean you up. No matter how confused or messed up, He will straighten you out. The process will hurt, but heaven is cheap enough at any price. This hope is so real that you can almost touch it.

I have mentioned that choosing to believe can be difficult. When I had my breakdown, the church became painfully aware of the unhealthy clutter of my brain. I had battled depression often but had escaped being labeled mentally ill. It can be a useless label that conjures up images of mental health facilities from the Middle Ages—dungeons and jails. If you are aware of your problems and seeking treatment, avoid labels that cripple. Don't let the diagnosis discourage you. By God's grace you will get better. If you actively seek His help, He will teach you how to manage, how to improve, and how to appreciate every small victory.

The church unintentionally labeled me mentally ill. I was crushed by their assumption that I wasn't getting help. I was crushed that they didn't understand that you don't recover from fifteen months of insomnia in a few weeks. I was crushed that they seemed indifferent to the trials of caring for a sick husband.

In my hurt, I was not fair to them, for they didn't know how to help. I should have been the one to teach that sort of thing and tell them my needs, but I was too exhausted. From my perspective, I felt that they considered me painfully out of sync with all that is good and holy. My behavior got worse. When you feel that the people you look up to have labeled you a loser, you don't try anymore. You throw in the towel and give way to meanness and despair.

This was when Bud stepped into my life. He seemed to be the one person who knew how badly I behaved and wasn't willing to give up on me. By faith he knew what God had for me. He encouraged every little improvement and tolerated no meanness in his presence. Allowing me to be a brat could only hinder his ability to help me. Appreciate and respect friends who are willing to set boundaries in your relationships. They can be very annoying, but these are the ones who are willing to be there for the long haul.

About a year later a friend told me I wasn't mentally ill. Her words carried some weight since she worked with mentally ill children. Then my psychiatrist told me the same thing a couple of days later. Hmm. He has knowledge and experience with me. Maybe they are onto something. The next day in church, Bud told me I wasn't mentally ill. I smiled. I believed it just that quickly. God sent three people who hadn't talked to each other to tell me I wasn't nuts. Yep. I was just fine, and with people believing in me, I started to act as if I wasn't nuts.

I want to make it clear that my church loves me. They tried to help me, and above all, they prayed for me. We all did the best we could with what we had at the moment.

Love is a powerful emotion. Love can motivate us to make all sorts of changes. As we grow in experience of God's love we can change destructive habits and thought patterns.

If we attach our affections to someone who isn't good for us, we can corkscrew our lives in a twisted, futile effort to please. In healthy relationships and healthy marriages, love expresses itself in a desire to see the other using gifts and talents in a fulfilling way.

One can live without romantic love. If you are a single parent, the most harmful thing you can do to yourself and the children is to hop from one romance to another. Even if you don't expose them to sexual abuse, the inability to make a commitment will damage them.

In all of our relationships, love is a choice. While we may have to move on when friends threaten to involve us in damaging behaviors, we should not ditch our friends easily. Commitment and respect are hallmarks of true love.

I have touched on the basic emotions. All of them must be expressed so that we can remain in control. Even love in a heterosexual friendship must be expressed. Express it publicly in ways that do not embarrass the other person. My husband actually preferred to be affectionately teased. Tell God of your love and ask Him to keep it holy and pure. Have many friends in order to keep the affection in perspective. As soon as a relationship seems forbidden and impure, it can turn into a romance of the devil. He loves to pollute anything that can be wholesome and beneficial.

If you are worried that a friend is having an emotional affair, be careful what you say. It is important to speak to that friend. It is damaging to talk to others about the situation. The more folks know, the harder it is to discreetly settle the situation. It is extremely dangerous to accuse the person of inappropriate thoughts when that person has said nothing along those lines. You can plant lust where there was none. Focus on behavior and how it appears to others. Your friend will feel less attacked and have an easier time benefiting from your words.

In a real comforter, the blocks are stitched neatly together. Each texture and color is confined tidily in place. Order and control reign smoothly.

Just try laying your feelings out in a row. Ha! Not even the God of the universe can do that. He made us to experience and to appreciate a multitude of emotions. He meant for us to feel many of them at once. Life can be a rainbow of emotion when we learn to express it.

A few years ago, I attended a woman's retreat. The weekend was a perfect blend of companionship and solitude. Solitude should not be feared. It can be a special time in His presence. It is important to building our relationship with God.

The first night the retreat didn't begin until late evening. Around five I wandered up to the hostess desk of the lodge's restaurant. The dining room was right on the waterfront. I was given a small table right by the picture window. The view was delightful, and I rejoiced at having such a fine table. Single diners don't often fare so well in fancy places.

As I studied the menu, I remembered the Riverfront Club in Columbus. Jerry and I had dined there on gift certificates he won through work. We savored every morsel and basked in each other's love. I was in a cheap black dress that made me look like a million bucks. We talked and laughed. We were lovers that night. We were not homeowners, or parents, or struggling financially. We were lovers and our eyes locked on the beauty of the evening.

I remembered another evening in southern Oregon. Dad, Jerry's father, took us to a supper club on the Rogue River. As he entertained us with his Alaskan adventures, I felt so pretty and cherished by these men who loved me.

Now back in Ohio and in the middle of nowhere, I felt many things. I rejoiced that I could remember Jerry and Dad so vividly. When I lose someone really close to me, I block their memory for a few months. Here I could mourn the separation that death had caused while cherishing the memories that God had given me. I felt a healthy pride over the doors God was opening for me. I enjoyed being able to feel so many emotions at once. It was a mile marker in my healing. Feelings are never tidy, but they are a great blessing. Surrendered to God, they help us cope. They help us relate to one another. Emotions can become common ground from which we can share how much Christ loves us.

Chapter 14

Relationships add color to the comforter of our lives. People make up the fluffy middle. This chapter focuses on how to relate to others in order to grow stronger and more like Christ.

Most of us have many opportunities to interact with others on a daily basis, both with friends and strangers.

When I am down, I give myself permission to be quiet. We do not have to fill every silence. In social and work situations, we do not have to hit the front door bubbling happiness and joy. A pleasant smile and frequent eye contact can set others at ease. A smile can make the difference between being labeled stuck up or just a little shy.

If you are feeling really scared, close your eyes and remember something happy. Now make yourself smile, and you will feel the tensions slide away. When you feel quiet, listen to the other person and ask God to help you care. Dwelling on your own problems 24/7 won't speed your healing. Listen and thank God for the opportunity to forget yourself.

Be cautious about investing in new relationships when you are down. Most of our friendships shouldn't center on our needs and healing. I could say that my friendship with Bud did center on that for a couple of years, but there always was an undercurrent that getting well included my becoming better able to help others.

No matter how down you are, God always places something in your pockets to share—a smile, a silent prayer, or gifts. Depression by its very nature draws us inward. While you must focus some of your energies on what you need to heal, a self-centered attitude can drive away the strongest people and frighten lesser mortals who may have originally thought that clinical depression was no big deal.

There are times when we need to be open about our struggle. Several years ago at a friend's dinner table, a young woman let into me for taking medication. "You are hiding behind pharmaceuticals instead of facing life."

I felt threatened. I prayed as I carefully chewed. It would have been easy to clam up, but I spoke. "These drugs replace chemicals that should have been in my brain in the first place. Now I can more effectively face my problems." In plain English, life with a sick husband was a serious game of poker. I wanted to play it with a full deck.

A month later she thanked me for speaking my mind. "I'm on medication now too, and it is helping me face my challenges." There are many misconceptions about depression and prescription drugs. As we heal, we should take advantage of the opportunities to educate those around us in an effort to make the way easier for those who follow. Remember, you don't need to spill all of your guts. In my depression, I confided too deeply in three people who felt it their duty to tell the rest of the church all of my business. I may be dealing with the repercussions from this for the rest of my life.

An important goal in dealing with others is to learn how to disagree agreeably. We do not need to feel threatened by those who disagree with us because the King of the universe stands right beside us. No matter how much someone might hammer us with advice, we don't have to take the advice. No one, not even God, can force us to do what we don't want to do. Ask God to show you if there is something to this person's words. If you speak softly, you are more likely to be heard.

When Jerry died, a young friend suggested that I move to the town where Kelly attended boarding school. What she didn't know is that she was asking me to sell my home and abandon my mother who lived nearby so that I could hover outside Kelly's dorm because staying in the dorm was part of Kelly's scholarship package. Gently I explained that to her and she quietly said, "I didn't know." End of advice.

No one likes to be hit over the head with another's opinion. A friend was bottle feeding her baby in public years ago. An older woman walked up to the baby and directed her comments to the infant. "Tell your mama that she has something better than that bottle." Mama blinked back the tears and didn't say that her baby was adopted. She took a defensive stand because she was cracked over the noggin by this stranger's opinion.

If we really want people to change for the better, we need to be gracious or filled with His grace. When we treat them as fellow strugglers in the game of life, we have honest communication. An added perk is that when we are dead wrong and gracious, we are more likely to be gently set straight.

Fear is a powerful emotion that can save lies or destroy rationality. It is good to be afraid to cross a busy street with your eyes closed. It can be lifesaving to be afraid of a gunman when you are a cashier at a convenience store. It is crippling to be so afraid of germs that you have to clean every doorknob before you can touch it. It is disastrous to be so fearful that you can't leave your house for anything.

Depression leaves us more fearful than normal. In our fear, we can cling to one friend with a death grip. I utterly destroyed a friendship that way. Jesus Christ is the only 24/7 Friend who can take a constant barrage of our needs without having to walk away to save Himself. He has an advantage. He is God. He did not come into the world to condemn it (John 3:17) so don't be afraid to come to Him. He wants you well, and He will never give up on you. His patience is endless. As we look to Him for guidance, He will send folks to us. He will help us to see that our friends also have needs.

Worry and fear can cause serious static in relationships. Dread can make us hear what we anticipate rather than what was said. This pulls the other person off balance and eventually the dust settles on one incredibly nasty brawl. Unchecked, worry and fear keep us from getting great advice from God in a timely fashion.

God can give you control over your fears, thoughts, and worries when you make listening to Him a priority. Some suggest that it is God's job to get our attention when He speaks. That is true when we don't know much about Him. The quality of our lives vastly improves as we learn to make listening to Him a priority. Life offers many distractions. By His grace we can eliminate some, control others and minimize the effects of the rest. This takes practice. We need to learn from our mistakes without beating ourselves up. We should be kind to ourselves as well as to others.

Sometime after Jerry died, I heard God whisper in a potentially disastrous situation. The church had started small group studies on *The Purpose Driven Life*. It took me weeks to get the courage to go. Although the church and I were on an even keel, I feared rubbing shoulders with my brothers and sisters in a small group.

One evening we came to the chapter about the church caring for its own. I still don't agree with Mr. Warren on this topic. He writes that the church should make a priority of caring for its own. In stark contrast I struggled through a breakdown and the care of a dying husband with minimal help from the church. In my isolation, God taught me most of the things Rick Warren put down in his book. In my plea for help, God sent others. As they helped me, I drew closer to God. Where my people failed, God blessed me beyond my wildest imagination. Because the church wasn't smothering me in attention, I had opportunities to tell my helpers about God.

With trepidation I shared this at the beginning of the discussion. One man told me my needs weren't being met because they were probably selfish. He fell back on this so often that I finally pointed out what had been said. Needing help caring for a dying spouse is not selfish. Bud had already witnessed to that. He also shut down some of my comments in an effort to protect me. We had no healing dialogue because everyone wanted me fixed as quickly as possible.

I excused myself because I had forgotten my book. "Wear your gloves? Do you have gloves? It is so cold out there," Bud admonished. In the hallway I gazed out into the early darkness and sent a young man after my book. I knew that if I got to my car I would probably drive off.

With the ice cold book in my hand I retreated to the dark safety of the sanctuary. "They don't get it. They just don't get it." I wept healing tears as I talked with God, the one person who always gets it. I then returned to the small group free to hear what was really said. My participation wasn't colored by past wounds or fear running wild. Afterwards Bud declared, "I'm so glad you got your book."

I could have laughed out loud. God gave me the power to inter-
pret man speak. The worry about my gloves meant, "We care about you."
Being glad about my getting my book meant, "I was relieved you didn't
run for the hills." Genuine love can exist even when understanding isn't
there.

Because I was learning to see from God's perspective, I was satis-
fied that I had tried to vent in a healthy manner. I was pleased that I could
graciously accept their inability to help without feeling rejected.

On Sabbath I sidled up to a woman from the group. I can't remember how I broached the subject or what possessed me to have another go
at it, but I will never forget her healing words. "I don't know what it feels
like to lose a husband, but it must have hurt terribly. It must have been
horrible to face his illness all alone." Praise God. Someone got it. God
used her to pull a splinter out of my heart. As a representative of the
church, she acknowledged my sufferings without casting blame on anyone.
When things are rough, blaming just spreads the misery.

Grief and loss can narrow our vision. We frequently connect these
two words with death. However, loss has a much broader scope. Loss can
include loved ones moving away, a decrease in physical or mental capaci-
ties, the loss of one's position in society, or the loss of a job. There is also
what is called disenfranchised loss. The pain is real, but it isn't acknowledged much by those around you. The death of a pet, a fiancé, or a dear
friend is often unnoticed.

Relationships can help us grow. Those with depression need to
be particularly careful not to focus on one or two people or to settle for
unhealthy relationships. A relationship is unhealthy if it focuses almost
exclusively on the needs of one person. This is true even when it is your
needs being met.

Any relationship based on belittling or degrading people is bad
news. While you are recovering from major depression, you may want to
put such relationships on the back burner. While you should avoid making
permanent or important decisions when you are really down, you have the
right to protect yourself and your mental balance. If these people truly
love you, they will be willing to learn healthy coping skills along with you
when you get a little better.

If you are a parent, you owe it to your children to learn how to
manage your depression as well as possible. When I had my breakdown,

I had friends on standby to take care of our daughter in case I was hospitalized. When I look back on it, if I had had to leave home, I would have wanted to tell Kelly myself that she had done nothing wrong. I would have told her everything was going to be fine whether I believed it or not. While you may have to stop being a caregiver to your children for a while, you never stop being a parent. Give them love. Even if it is a struggle, try to think of someone other than yourself.

I read an article on arthritis a while back. It recommended keeping as active as possible. Depression reduces our ability to think of others. We need to keep as active as possible. If you ask, God will show you something congenial to your tastes, talents, and current abilities. When Jerry was sick, I would embroider for hours and share the fruits of my needle with friends and family. I was not up to working in a soup kitchen or solving the world's problems, but jt was something I could do to keep from drawing inward and feeling sorry for myself.

Good relationships are vital to a healthy, productive life.

Chapter 15

Accountability is an unseen concept that is vital to a usable comforter or a functional life. Its absence is way more noticeable than its presence.

When Kelly graduated high school she did so with four others who had gone to school with her since grade school. I used six-inch blocks and zipped them together into sixteen rows of sixteen blocks. This makes a square 81 inches by 81 inches. What if in the middle of the project I had decided to use four-inch blocks? Worse yet, what if I lost my ruler and my template and had to guess.

If I had screwed up the comforter, I'm sure the graduate would have politely thanked me and maybe even given me a hug. She would have probably scratched her head and wondered how I did it. How did I make it so lumpy, so wrinkled, so cockeyed looking? A person without a sense of accountability has trouble with even the most basic survival skills. I have met people in prison who landed there simply because they couldn't follow the basic rules of their probation. They were not hindered by addictions. They just couldn't follow rules.

Accountability is vital to managing depression well. Simple, healthy friendships elude a person who refuses to be held accountable for his behavior. In my sewing I use a ruler and a tape measure. In my life, I rely on the Bible and friends who also measure themselves by the Bible. In reference to managing depression, I have a few close friends who know what I deal with and understand my goals. For example, my daughter knows that she is welcome to correct my manners because I really don't want to be an embarrassment. She does this so gracefully that it is better than looking like an oaf. Once when friends were near, she whispered in my ear and took a moment to caress my hair. No one knew she was keeping me from being gross in public.

My goal in life is to be like Jesus Christ because He loved me enough to leave the safety and comfort of heaven. The more we realize how much He loves us, the more appealing are His ways of doing things. While this seems like a tall order, it is just like anything else worth striving for. You thank God for each half inch of progress. When you fall back three inches, you dust yourself off and thank Him that it wasn't four inches. If you fall off the path altogether, you can call out for His help and count on it.

Honesty without brutality is one of His ways. I shared a lot of my feelings with Bud. I needed a safe place to express those feelings so I could move on. Even to this day he is a great source for reality checks. If I am right, he says so. If I am blowing a problem out of proportion, he doesn't blindly sympathize with me. Friends too eager to take my side have done me more harm than those who have written me off as a loss.

A Beautiful Mind is a movie about John Nash, a Nobel prize winning mathematician. Despite schizophrenia he made a significant contribution to economic theory. He mathematically proved what the Bible supports: What's good for the many is good for the few. I want friends who encourage me to postpone my immediate needs for the good of the many. In the long run, we're all happier for it.

Sexual purity does much to promote our happiness. God invented sex and marriage. If you think He is a prude, read Song of Solomon in the

Bible. He wants us to experience pleasure in the context of a marriage relationship. Marriage is meant to illustrate how He loves His bride, the church. The church is all who follow Jesus Christ regardless of where they worship. Sexual promiscuity makes it hard for us to see what God is like. Promiscuity implies that God is fickle and changeable in choosing whom He loves. Instead, He loves us simply because we are. Nothing we do can change how much He loves us.

What is perversion? (See Leviticus 20:7–21.) Perversion means a deviation from God's perfect will for our lives, particularly in the realm of sex. Same-sex relations, incest, and beastiality distort His image in our relationships. Discovering that they are sinful doesn't take away the desire for them. However, Christ can change our desires and give us the power to do and enjoy His will (2 Corinthians 10:5).

If you are caught up in practices that conflict with God's plan for your sex life, He still loves you. Nothing you can do nor anything that has been done to you will make Him stop loving you. He will heal you and restore you. He will show you how to change your life and give you the cour-age to do it.

Keep the Ten Commandments (Exodus 20:1–18). Love God with all your heart because He already loves you. Don't let anything get between you and God. Don't love your money or things so much that you would sin in order to get them. Don't allow your friends to make you uneasy about your friendship with God. An idol is anything you love more than God.

Keep the Sabbath. The only way we keep any of the commandments is by resting in what He has already done for us. The Sabbath reminds us of that. Don't murder—don't take a life or demean someone with words designed to ruin self-esteem. Everyone is made by God, and that alone makes us valuable. Honor your parents so that you can live long in the land. Even your parents are valued by God. They brought you into the world. If you don't appreciate that now, wait a while.

If they have been harmful to you, forgive them. If they remain harmful to you, put much prayer into the decision to limit or eliminate your contact with them. Sometimes that truly must happen. Praying about the decision will give you peace.

Do not commit adultery. Marriage is supposed to be a little fortress that makes us feel safe regardless of what is going on around us. It illustrates God's unwavering love for us. Don't mess with that. If you have, ask His forgiveness and that of your spouse. His ability to restore what we have broken is amazing. Don't be quick to throw in the towel. Don't steal. Don't lie. Don't covet because it leads to other sins.

The commandments show us who God is. He is honest and faithful. Obedience to them isn't some arbitrary act of compliance to appease an all-powerful bully. These rules are designed to keep all of us happy and safe. One day a friend let his junior high class function without rules. It was one of the last things he did at that school. By the end of the day, the class was begging for rules. The complete absence of rules kept each student from enjoying the particular rule he wanted to break. One girl couldn't enjoy her novel because of the noise. Another student couldn't enjoy his graffiti on the chalkboard because another had erased it as quickly as he could write. Another used his freedom to pick up after everyone else. He disliked the absence of rules so much that he felt compelled to restore order bit by bit. Not only has God made the rules for the good of the many, He also stands ready to say, "Here, let Me give you a hand with that," when we struggle and feel it is impossible to obey.

Pornography breaks many rules. While looking at it, you covet what isn't yours, and your fantasies are a lie. You have contributed to the theft of virtue. You support an industry that is frequently based on forcing people to participate against their will. You murder in the sense that you contribute to the degradation of many. Get out of it now. Once those images are in your mind, you may very well remember them vividly for the rest of your life, whether you want to or not.

Substance abuse is another problem that keeps us from having healthy, happy lives. Accountability to God and man are vital to breaking addictions. When you decide to leave an unhealthy behavior behind, God becomes your own private cheerleader. He gladly praises every step in the right direction no matter how small it is. He patiently dusts you off and cleans your wounds when you fall. He knows we are weak and will give us all the help we ask for. If you are willing, He will show you how to remove yourself from the path of temptation.

When you fall, don't beat yourself up. God made you, and He doesn't make junk. Don't give up because you are well worth the battle. No matter how dirty and ugly your life has been, no matter what has been done to you, claim God's everlasting love for you. Your persistence will help you become a marvel of God's handiwork.

God's commandments are a little like playground rules. You can break them now and then and "get away" with it. A little lie here or helping yourself to a little something that isn't yours often goes unnoticed. However, the principle behind these little sins is the real danger. When we think His law is unimportant or unattainable, we develop a dangerous attitude. We start believing it doesn't matter and that we can get away with it. We push and shove to get what we want. Eventually someone gets seriously injured.

Shock and remorse dog our every waking moment. Yes, Christ forgives. Yes, He saves or restores. Still, the process can be long and painful. In our lives we will hurt enough people even when we do all in our power to avoid it. Willful disobedience does serious damage to our psyches. Our actions teach our loved ones more powerfully than our words. Do we really want our children to sink to our level? Wouldn't it be better if our behavior pointed them to a loving God who has principles for their happiness?

In the same spirit of willfulness that kept me from getting psychiatric help in a timely fashion, I butted against God's will for my life. I was clever. I was smart. I didn't need all the rules. I still bear scars in my heart. I hope these scars do not go away until He returns. Why do I want them? They remind me to stay close to God. They remind me to want His rules for my safety and those around me. They make me more effective at helping others.

Some of the lessons He taught me in that dark, bitter time were things He had been trying to teach me for twenty years. I wish I could say that I just didn't get it. The great consolation is that God can take our painful experiences and use them to shape us and to help others. I am lucky. I was able to make peace with all of the people I hurt. All forgave me. We need to forgive. We can't always reconcile. Sometimes we have to let go of those whom we have hurt. We may have so bewildered or frightened them that this is the kindest thing we can do.

Christ is willing to give us everything we need to obey His law. He will even help us want to obey if we ask for that. However, He will not force our will. If we express to Him even the weakest desire to improve, He will grow that desire into a healthy pattern of thought.

You can't be happy if you don't hold yourself accountable to some sort of standard. If you select God's standards, forgiveness is built in. Remember how I make my comforters with six-inch blocks? They aren't perfect. You will see a tuck here or a wrinkle there where a block was too long. You may see where I cut through a row of blocks because my backing wasn't just the right size. I make comforter rather than quilts because a comforter is more forgiving. Because there is more stitching in a quilt, accuracy is more important. Our lives are like comforters. Forgiveness is built in if we accept it.

Chapter 16

Believe it or not (since I've used it as an analogy for life), I'm not real fond of making comforters. Much of the work is repetitious. My graduation comforters required hours of what I consider factory work—zip, zip, zip. The blocks march through the sewing machine. Now they are strips and sometime soon I will have to press open the seams and do more sewing. I don't like sewing comforters. But I do like hearing, "You did all this work for me?" That's what my sister Louise said to me when I brought one to her in her new home in Florida. I've been hooked every since.

How do we endure depression? It's just like a marathon. There are tricks to enduring and enjoying. Sometimes I reward myself for chores I don't want to do. When I was a full-time homemaker, laundry day wasn't my favorite. Every time I emptied the dryer and put the clothes away, I put up my feet and read until the next load was dry.

Treat yourself when you complete something unpleasant. Consider your treats carefully. If healthy eating is a problem in your life, you may want to steer away from sweets as a reward. A walk in the park without the children or fifteen minutes of uninterrupted reading may do the trick. Perhaps there is something you enjoy more. I find embroidery a peaceful treat at the end of a hectic day. I have a gift for stretching a buck.

Sometimes shopping at a thrift store yields an affordable treasure. I also consider fresh produce a treat.

Coping with clinical depression is similar to running a marathon. You do all you can to avoid the blues—eat right, sleep well, exercise, and take medications according to directions. By the way, alcohol is a depressant, and I recommend leaving it alone altogether. Still you have your down days. There are many coping strategies for avoiding them or surviving them gracefully.

First, keep your life simple. Buy clothing that is easy to care for. You can dress well and rarely see a dry cleaner. Try to have a place for everything, and leave everything in its place. The more important the items are, the higher the priority for putting them away every time you use them. Legal documents and car keys fall under that category. Multiple copies of inexpensive items can make life easy. Every January I stock up on gloves that have been marked down. If you buy several pairs of one color, it makes life very easy.

Honesty is another form of simplicity. Tell the truth. This doesn't have to be a detailed exposé of the objectionable. If someone asks, "Do you like my outfit?" consider the circumstances. How close is the person to you? Can they change, or are you already out in public? Most of the time, I just stick with anything encouraging and honest.

Another form of honesty is recognizing who you are. Don't overestimate your good qualities or whitewash your faults (Philippians 2:1–16). God loves you as is. He thinks you are wonderful. He can better help you when you choose honesty. He can't help you improve if you insist that you are just fine.

In His love you can always find the security you need in order to be honest about your faults. Writing this book has been the most difficult project I have ever undertaken. I have had to keenly remember what the breakdown was like. I've been stumbling through dark memories and asking friends to keep this project in their prayers. I had to take a three-week break when writing the original manuscript. When I told Bud about this break, it was the one time he seemed upset with me. "You stopped?" He startled me so much that I went straight home from church, ate leftovers at the computer, and finished the book. Sometimes there is nothing like a good swift kick in the hindquarters.

God is your friend. Learn to confide in Him through prayer. Prayer just means talking to God. When you read your Bible, look for how much God loves you. Ask Him to show you that. Ask Him for wisdom and strength. He will generously give you every good thing you need to live healthy and happy. If the answer to your prayer looks like no, this is what He really means: "Watch what I am going to do. I am about to shock your socks off!"

Simplify your life by avoiding debt. This is so important that I have an entire chapter on money and possessions. Here I will mention that there are organizations such as Consumer Credit Counseling that will help you avoid filing for bankruptcy. Negotiating with your creditors for lower interest rates and a suspension of penalties is a form of honesty. God will bless your efforts to pay what you owe. Bankruptcy should be considered a last resort rather than the first option.

Sometimes things happen. You lose your job. You are single and none of your family is in a position to help. You get sick and don't have health insurance. Don't be ashamed if you are in debt. Get help now. Jerry and I had several thousand dollars in credit card debt going for most of our marriage. Since I handled the checkbook, it was a horrible strain on me.

Simplify your life by choosing your battles carefully. When Jerry was really sick, I had so many problems come at me that I stopped worrying. I wish I could say I was brilliantly wise and chose not to worry. I could only watch God open doors and sometimes punch holes in walls and whisper, "Come here!"

Will this problem matter two days from now? Will it matter a year from now? Does it have any bearing on your plan to be with God forever? Is there anything you can do about this situation that worries you? Have you done what you can? Worry can be like picking at a scab. A little can be helpful because it moves you to do what you can. A lot can keep the problem from resolving itself.

Experience makes things easier. Be patient with yourself if you are doing something new. It takes courage to try new things. If you don't do something new now and then, how will you ever gain experience? The more experience I have with those dark days, the better I know that I can survive them gracefully.

When you are down, try to do just a little more than you want to. Make yourself get out of bed. Do a little housework. Make yourself sit outside in the sunshine even if you have to bundle up to do it. Each day do a little something you don't want to do but you know is good for you or others. Give friends and family permission to push you a little. When friends learned that I was marrying a diabetic, some took the stance that suddenly I was completely responsible for his eating habits. He had been diabetic for seven years, but now I was supposed to boss him as if he were two years old. I didn't buy into that because I wanted our marriage to last more than a year. As he decided changes were necessary, I supported him and did all I could to encourage him in the changes he chose.

Praising God helps light up the darkness. If life seems like one problem after another, God is still God. Praise Him for who He is. He doesn't change. He is loving, good, and kind regardless of how your day is going. He is eager to teach you and carry you even when you cannot sense His presence. Keep talking to Him. He invites us to reason with Him. The more we dialog with Him, the more opportunities He has to train us how to think more positively. It still astounds me how much He has taught me since the breakdown. Now when something doesn't go as planned, I quickly see what can be learned from it. I am more likely to see the failure as a steppingstone toward what I want to accomplish.

Every time you try something new, pat yourself on the back. Every time you feel like a failure, step back. Take a deep breath and grab God's hand. Ask Him, "What did I do right? What did I learn here?"

When my parents were kids, merry-go-rounds had brass rings on the outside of the circle. If you rode one of the outside animals, you were allowed to stretch and grab the brass ring. You won a free ride this way. Winning wasn't for the timid. You needed to be willing to stand in the stirrups and stretch with your whole body.

Every time you try something new, you are reaching for the brass ring. Every time you push yourself a little, you are going for the gold. You are adding solid, brilliant blocks to the comforter of your life. If the block is less than perfect, it makes your comforter unique. If you miss the brass ring, you still have gained confidence and wisdom for having tried. You do not have to try something new every day, but celebrate each attempt. There is value in just trying.

Work is vital to coping with depression. Whether it is volunteer work, save-the-family-money work, or a paying job outside the home, we are all meant to do useful work that benefits others. While paychecks are beneficial, they shouldn't be the main reason why you work. Be a blessing to your employer by doing the best you can. Try to be cheerful. Once a coworker asked me how I felt. "Good. Well, that's not true, but if I keep saying it, I will feel better." Keep smiling. It may not drive the blues away, but it will help make the darkness bearable.

Your work environment should be healthy. Sexual harassment is often in the eyes of the beholder. If someone says or does anything that makes you uncomfortable, your duty is to tell that person to stop it. They may say they meant no harm by it. Give them the benefit of the doubt when it comes to motive. If they stop doing what makes you uncomfortable, it doesn't matter what is in the heart. That's God's concern. If step one doesn't work, go to a supervisor. If that person is the supervisor, go to the boss.

Try not to be combative. This sort of thing can be embarrassing to everyone involved. Remaining calm can help the problem to be resolved quickly and kindly. What you find creepy may be normal and wholesome in that person's family. Some families kiss everyone on the lips. Some folks are all hugs. Others need their personal space.

You also have the right to be treated with courtesy and kindness in the workplace and a duty to do likewise regardless of how you are treated. If you are in a bad work environment, ask God to show you if you can change it or if you just need to move on. When management encourages or condones disrespect toward employees that may be your cue to leave.

Sometimes anger needs to be expressed in the workplace. Stick to the subject. An action or deed may be stupid, thoughtless, or dangerous, but the person isn't stupid or bad. We all have our moments. If we discuss behavior, it is easier for the person to correct behavior because they aren't put on the defensive. Sometimes I have to sit on my anger for a day or two while I try to figure out how to express it in a healthy manner. However, the sooner you can get it off your chest in a healthy manner, the better for everyone.

Another way to keep life simple is to stick with the issue at hand when you are angry. It is hard to sit still while you get a tongue lashing. Don't dredge up every objectionable thing the person has ever done, particularly if those problems have been settled. None of us can improve if our past mistakes are constantly rehashed. If you are getting into frequent arguments with someone who really doesn't want to change, you need to rethink the relationship. Can you be an example of unconditional love to this person? Are their behaviors a serious threat to your well-being? For example, if I were a recovering alcoholic, I would avoid people who drink in my presence and try to coerce me into joining them.

With Christ we can endure all things. If we cannot endure, He provides a way of escape (1 Corinthians 10:13). When problems seem insurmountable, I look at it from another angle. I tell God, "Well, this wouldn't be happening if we couldn't tackle it." God is your forever Friend, and He will help you endure and grow more beautiful, wise, and helpful every day. There will be days when it seems as if there is no growth. That's okay. He is preparing you for great things. Do not be overwhelmed by all the advice in this chapter. Ask God to order your days and show you what to do moment by moment. Not all changes come quickly. Pat yourself on the back each time you try to improve or learn something new.

Chapter 17

Cha-ching! I love that sound. Jerry used to say that when I was making good tips as a waitress my eyes would twinkle tiny dollar signs. Money is a useful tool, but the love of money is a sin (1 Timothy 6:10). Loving money means that you are so interested in it that you will do anything to get it and may just hoard it away when you have it.

When I moved out on my own after college, I began to return a tithe to God. In the Old Testament this money supported the priesthood. In my denomination, this 10 percent supports the clergy. It is distributed throughout the world so that a pastor with a little church eats just as well as one managing a huge congregation. Also, if a pastor's income isn't strictly dependent on his home church, he is free to preach the Word of God even if it might offend some of the local leadership. He can be honest and not worry about his next meal.

Tithing is a demonstration of your trust that God will take care of you. When I put my check in the offering plate, no matter how big or small, I am saying to Him, "My job is to obey You. Your job is to make sure I eat." Tithe is between God and me. If the church misuses it, He takes care of it. That's His job too. Regardless of what the church does, He still blesses me for this demonstration of faith because that is between the two of us (Malachi 3:10). It is not a guarantee that you will never pay a bill late or always be neck deep in all the stuff you could possibly want. However, my experience has been that I always have enough and some to share. Also, the more I share, the more there is for me.

Tithing is not a free pass to neglect managing your money. Budgeting is a good idea. I can't say much about it because I have never had a formal budget. It is hard when you bring home most of your income in one-dollar bills. I did this for twenty-five years as a waitress. When I was single the first time, I budgeted by priorities. Rent was due at the end of the month. On the first I started setting aside the rent money to deposit into checking. Utilities were the next priority. I'd fill each envelope with tips. Those were the good old days. I would walk downtown to pay them in person. During those two or three weeks, I didn't buy many groceries or extras unless I was making really good progress on my priorities.

I was cheap so there was never much of an entertainment budget. Each time I got a paycheck I used the stub to figure out my tithe and placed that anount in the offering plate the next Sabbath. I declared all of my tips. Now that I'm counting down the years to retirement, I'm very glad I declared all of my income.

As you regain your mental strength, seek out friends who seem to handle their money well. There are many things that help me live beyond my means without being in debt. Debt is a form of stress. The less debt you have the better off you are. I am debt free at the moment. I praise God and consider it a miracle. If you are reckless with a credit card, leave it at home. If you are a compulsive buyer, cancel the account. Cash has become a really inconvenient way to buy a number of things, but it beats mega debt and the inconvenience of bankruptcy.

Clearance is my favorite brand. This is how I can get a brand new blouse for a dollar. You can find everything on clearance now. I've gotten soap, dishes, paper plates, and greeting cards this way. I've seen God give me just the right thing at the right time on the clearance shelf or rack. Sometimes I have wondered why on earth I bought something on clearance at a good price to see that the item turned out to be important. Then I tell God, "A-ha. You knew just what I needed before I did."

Many of the blocks in my comforters come from clothing or cloth that was given to me. I hate cutting up clothes, but sometimes there is a stain or a rip that cannot be fixed. Learn to mend and fix your clothes. It can save you a bundle, and it isn't too hard. Accept hand-me-downs. Some of the finest clothing I've ever owned were hand-me-downs, nicer than I could have afforded on my income.

Don't hoard your stuff. Two years after my breakdown, I was well enough to clean out the attic. I had so much sewing stuff up there that I no longer knew what I had. At that point I thought I would never sew again. I had no idea that God would restore that gift and kick it into overdrive. For then I took carload after carload of stuff to the Salvation Army. When I was ready to sew again, God blessed me with an ever-increasing stash.

Give and you will receive in return (Luke 6:38). This isn't a tit-for-tat philosophy. If you help someone, don't expect payback from that person. God is willing to order your days. He will teach you how to use it up, make do, or do without. He will also honor your desire to live as debt free as possible. (I believe that a car and a house are worth going into debt for.) As you seek to help others with your stuff, God will bless you. Although there may be tight times, He will meet your needs and delight you now and then with the stuff you really want. As tight as things have been over the years, I have never lacked for pretty clothing to wear. He dresses me as splendidly as the lilies of the field (Luke 12:27).

Rent to own is the most expensive way to buy anything. If you are establishing your own household, there are many things you don't have to have immediately. You can set up household with a mattress, box spring, table, and a chair. A few dishes and pots and pans from a thrift store will keep you out of restaurants and give you more money to put into your household. Don't be afraid of garage sales and rummage sales. Some of my best pieces of furniture were bought used. It is hard to find and afford that kind of quality new.

Making do can help you do without. A dish towel or a bath towel on the kitchen counter can substitute for a dish drainer. A towel on the kitchen table isn't the perfect ironing board but it works well enough to keep you from buying everything at once. A fork handle stuck in a drinking glass makes a nice recipe card holder. Conversation and books make nice replacements for the TV set you can't afford. Once you get the TV, do you really need cable or satellite? The public library has loads of tapes and

DVDs on a variety of subjects. You can even catch up on your favorite TV shows. You can find shows that will help you learn simple skills that save you money. Sewing and simple home improvements are the first things that come to mind.

Having an orderly home decreases stress. If you can't afford dressers, get some boxes. Tomato boxes and chicken cases make sturdy, free storage units. To this day I use them for storage supplies. Tubberware is my favorite for food storage. Yes, that is T-U-B-B-E-R-W-A-R-E. When you buy food in plastic containers, reuse them. Once you have a well-equipped kitchen you can toss them. I always save some for leftovers to send with a guest. Then there is no hassle returning the dish. For my own kitchen I tend to put leftovers in glass dishes and cover with plastic wrap. That makes it easier to see what I have, and I can eat out of the dish without feeling totally uncouth.

When I freeze leftovers, I tend to dump them into zippered bags. Again, I can see what I have. Bread bags make cheap freezer bags. I put baked goods right into them because a few breadcrumbs won't hurt. When I freeze things for later use, I put the food in cheap plastic bags and then place those bags in bread bags. The double wrap eliminates freezer burn. If I'm freezing something in the store wrap, I wrap it up in a plastic shopping bag. Plastic shopping bags also make good trash can liners. People tidier than I am may wish to invest in good quality liners for the kitchen garbage.

Everything in your home doesn't have to be just so immediately. If it all looks shabby enough, friends and family will never have to strain their brains regarding what to get you for Christmas.

Make up your mind to value freedom from debt more than having nice things. If you don't get everything new right away, you will better value what you have. You will have a collection of wonderful stories about how God provided your stuff. My best dishes were given to me by my mother ages ago. They were a clearance item I casually admired in the store where she worked. She surprised me with them on New Year's Day. They are often mistaken for more expensive china.

Learn to cook. Rent DVDs from the library. Get recipes from the Internet. Often I save money by typing my available ingredients into a recipe site's search engine. That way when I get plantains for a quarter a pound they don't go to waste. They were delicious pan fried and served with a little lime juice. If there isn't much time to cook and eat with your family, cook ahead and microwave. Load up the crockpot in the morning. Plan ahead so that you can eat healthy rather than filling up on junk food while scrambling to make supper.

Chapter 18

Our lives change whether we want them to or not. A new job, moving, or a death in the family means changes in our routine. When those things happen to people in your network, it changes your routine too. While I am fairly strong and healthy, aging requires me to change how I do things. For example, a fifty-pound sack of potatoes gets divvied up out in the garage and carried in as two bags. Change is like an empty room you have never seen before. You decide what you bring with you. Sometimes the room is dark and unknown. This makes it harder to know what to bring. The death of a spouse or a disabling illness are examples of dark rooms. Other rooms are well lit and easier to negotiate. Getting married, having a baby, or landing the job you've tried so hard to get are brightly lit rooms.

All these new rooms represent stress. Even minor changes create some stress and can be very challenging when you are depressed. I reorganized my china cabinet. A month later I was fussing because I couldn't find a particular set of bowls. When I finally calmed my mind, I remembered that I had moved them to the microwave stand. I was red-faced because I accused Kelly of dragging them off to odd corners of the house and forgetting them. Now, I have found some whopper collections of mold in my favorite dishes when they were left in the attic by my dear daughter, so my mind wasn't exactly running wild.

Since then I've been more careful about reorganizing the house. I do a little here and there in the hope of remembering the changes. I do this stuff on days I feel sharper. All this is an argument for owning less stuff. I firmly believe that the more you own, the more likely it is to own you.

Some changes are not by choice. If Jerry and I had a say, he would be alive and well. A friend really startled me at the calling hours before Jerry's funeral. She was young and inexperienced. She wanted me to pack my bags and move to the town where Kelly was attending boarding school. I mentioned that I owned by house free and clear and that Kelly's scholarship included boarding fees. I was too flabbergasted to mention my aged mother who lived only three miles away. I did well considering I wanted to scream, "I am widowed! Why would I want to take on rent or a mortgage in a town where I don't know anyone?"

When you are dealing with something major like a death in the family, avoid making big changes. The best and brightest of us can make stupid decisions when grief clouds our judgment. Stick to minor changes for now, if possible. My mother changed her television viewing after Papa died. She started watching baseball and science fiction because she enjoyed them but he hadn't.

When Jerry was sick, there were so many changes we had no control over. For his surgery, he was supposed to be out of the hospital in a week and back to work in six months. He was in the hospital for a month. From day to day we never knew if he would come home or not. Up until the very end of that stay, they talked of placing him in a nursing home.

I learned to carve out a routine in the chaos. Each morning at home I would read the Bible and pray. I would go to the hospital and stay with Jerry until it was time to be at work around 11 a.m. I returned to the hospital around 2 p.m. We lived only ten minutes away from the hospital, so going home for a few minutes to check the mail helped me cope. Jerry always wanted me to go home by 10 p.m., even if he was in the ER. He knew I needed my rest, and he didn't begrudge me. If I had to do it all over again with someone less understanding, I would insist on leaving by ten o'clock.

I probably wouldn't have spent so much time with Jerry except we both rested or relaxed more in each other's presence. He dozed whenever he wanted, and his care seemed better because I could communicate with the staff. If he was uncomfortable, he would tell me rather than bother the staff. Sometimes he was too confused to communicate well, and I could guess his needs simply because we had been together so long.

I guess what I am trying to say is that in all the changes Jerry's illness brought we found peace in continuing to keep each other company. Sometimes when faced with bigger changes we cope best by focusing on what hasn't changed. Every time we laughed together, I thanked God we could still do that.

Waiting is another stressful thing. Sometimes we wait to see the doctor. Especially if it is nothing serious, we would just love to get the appointment done and get on with our lives. Most of my adult life I had a doctor who ran his office like a train station. You got in on time, and you got treated. He then planted his feet when he asked you if you had any questions. He put last-minute appointments at the end of the day to minimize the inconvenience. Dear Dr. Davis was a treasure. Now I have to wait. Reading or needlework helps. Sometimes I catch up on paperwork.

I did a lot of waiting when Jerry was ill. Part of the time I was waiting for him to die. It was like straining your ears at night to hear the other shoe drop. We can waste a whole lifetime waiting. We wait for the right job. We wait for a good mate. We wait for the winning lottery ticket. We wait for everything to be perfect so we can be happy. We anticipate trouble. We look ahead for joy. Sometimes I ask God to help me enjoy today because the past is gone and the future hasn't arrived. Now is only a moment, but it is ours. We must enjoy the present as best we can.

When Kelly was five, we started to go to roller skating rinks. She had already learned on sidewalks, and I had learned as a teen. We went every week. I still have my skates from then. They are white boots with bright pink wheels. I can skate forward, and my command of the toe stop is enough to be dangerous. Despite that, Kelly and I enjoyed going to the rink. Everything around us stopped while we skated for a couple of hours.

The secret to waiting is to find a way to enjoy now. I bring a good book or a bit of embroidery. I start a conversation in the checkout line. I savor the scenery rolling by my car window when I have a long drive. A really long drive may require an audio book from the library. On one long car trip I started writing this book in my head. For this edition, I started editing in my head while cutting fabric.

We have talked about changes in character, shaping our lives to desire good. When a lot is changing around us and we are stressed out, we may easily slip into old habits. We need to be patient with ourselves then. When we are talking of lifelong habits such as negative thinking or profanity, we can easily slip off the straight and narrow. There will be more temptation to return to dangerous addictions when life is a little more than we can comfortably handle. Pray for strength. Pray for wisdom. Ask God to protect you from temptation. Don't underestimate the power of friends who pray. Forgive yourself for a misstep. Don't beat yourself up. Don't carry on about being stupid and worthless.

Ask His forgiveness. Remember that you are still priceless to God. Since He forgives you, you have no right to refuse to forgive yourself. When we struggle with depression, change comes inch by inch. It is best measured by looking back. Where were you six months ago? How much have you grown in a year? Treasure each step forward and don't let the steps backward discourage you. If you let God lead, you will be just fine.

Chapter 19

This chapter is about parenting. I hate the subject. When Kelly was growing up, I got plenty of criticism regarding my parent skills. Now that she is grown, has a healthy family, holds down a job, and doesn't abuse drugs, everyone thinks I did a fine job. They forget Jerry had a huge impact on her success. So whether you think I'm mother of the year or a self-centered woman who should never have had a child, I'm going to give you advice. I think the one thing I got right was choosing who, besides Jerry, would help us raise her.

Children whose values are instilled by a community have a stronger set of values. Children from split homes are often told they don't have to listen to the other parent because "they have no right to boss you." This undermines the sense of authority and respect that children need. Once I waited on a family while the restaurant was really busy. As I unloaded my tray of drinks, the little girl started to reach for hers. Because I didn't want to bathe the family in soda, I sternly asked her to wait. The mother decided I was mean to her baby. I was scolded right in front of the six-year-old. I turned the table over to another waitress. I explained to the family that I realized I had offended them and felt they would enjoy their meal more if they had another server. Every time I passed that table, the little girl loudly proclaimed that she didn't have to listen to me because I was mean to her. When they left, the dad looked very sheepish. He had learned an important lesson. I prayed that the mom had too.

For the sake of everyone's mental health, we need to respect authority. We need to teach our children that adults can be gruff or stern and still merit our respect. We don't have to agree with others completely in order to respect them.

Learning to take it on the chin a little here and there for the sake of order doesn't hurt. This may offend our sense of individuality, but the good of the many needs to come first. It doesn't take away from the good of the few. If a teacher is trying to cover a lesson, who will learn if a few are allowed to argue about their test grade during the lesson? If children sass and talk back during gym, someone may get hurt because they couldn't hear the instructions. This carries over to the workplace. This doesn't create mindless robots. One of the best things I taught Kelly was how to disagree politely. This includes kindness and waiting until an appropriate time to speak up. Usually this means talking one on one.

When we are not coping well with life, we need to let our children in on it. The younger they are, the more careful we must be not to give them information they cannot handle. "I don't feel well. I need to go away to get better and be able to take care of you. I love you very much." This is plenty enough when you are severely depressed. As the kids grow older, don't hide from them what happened. Your breakdown or hospitalization is shameful only if they hear about it in hushed tones from people who think it is shameful. Clinical depression often runs in families. You do your children a big favor if you show them that there is no shame in getting help. If you can teach them to have healthy attitudes toward life, they may be able to avoid medication.

There is no shame in getting help. Remember that. There is no shame in getting help. This is important. As you try to restore balance in your life, associate with people who firmly believe that. Avoid people who want you to hide your condition from everyone. Associate with people who tend to remain calm no matter what. When you are upset about a problem, you don't need people who will contribute to your turmoil.

Because of the moral climate we live in, I felt obliged to teach Kelly about molestation before she could quite understand. It is okay to talk a little over your children's heads. They understand more than we realize.

Just remember to be patient when they don't understand. Most children are very bright. The trick is to answer questions in ways they will understand. Teach them patience. "Give me a minute to think of the answer" or "Let me think of the right words" were phrases that left Kelly unafraid to ask questions and kept me from losing patience with both of us.

Here are the words I gave Kelly about molestation. I told her she shouldn't talk to strangers and she should stay close to the adult she was with. I told her not to scream if she was carried off. "If you scream, people will think you are just having a temper tantrum. If you yell loudly and clearly that this isn't your mom or dad, people will pay attention." I taught her where strangers shouldn't touch her and that she should make a lot of noise if they tried to do these things. Since then I heard a police officer say to a group of children, "If the person makes the hair on the back of your neck stand up, get away from him." I thought that was a great statement. All these things protect your children without undermining their sense of authority.

Tell your children that nothing done to them can make them bad. "Sometimes when people touch you where they shouldn't, they tell you not to tell anyone. They tell you that they will hurt Mommy or Daddy. They can't do that. God protects us. If you keep this all to yourself, you hurt more and more. Nothing anyone can do to you will ever make us stop loving you. We will always love you." Of course, all this coaching was spread out over a few years. The tone was matter-of-fact so as not to frighten her.

It is important to show this love when they tell you they did something wrong. Praise their honesty. Reward them by not getting upset or out-of-control over what they did. If it was direct disobedience, punish them. However, remain calm. It takes courage for a little one to admit they did wrong. Honesty is an important character trait. If we learn to lie really well, we never grow and improve ourselves. We never have to admit our faults. We never have to get help because we can constantly con ourselves into believing everything is fine. Honesty is important to sanity.

Verbal and physical abuse often occur when one or both parents are depressed. It takes energy and the ability to think quickly to use strategies more effective than yelling or hitting. Yes, it is shameful to be beating up on your kids or intimidating them with your words. But it is a greater shame not to get help. Don't wait for children's services to come looking for you. If you have a good network of friends and family, you can have a say where the children go. Your children have a right not to live in fear of you. By God's grace, you can give them that. Telling your children that your words or actions were inappropriate does not undermine their respect for authority An occasional lapse in judgment merits an apology. You can do this without giving the child a free pass to disobey.

The result of sexual abuse is horrendous. It destroys trust and thus can destroy the concept of a loving God who really cares. Most children (boys and girls) who are abused live in a home where the daddy isn't there biological father. Ladies, when you hop from live-in to live-in boyfriend, you expose your children to untold harm. If you can't make it on your own, consider giving up the children or sharing a home with a stable family. This can be another single woman.

Don't put the false sense of security of having a man before the safety and emotional well being of your children. If you can't control yourself, give the children up. Foster care and adoption agencies aren't perfect, but the odds are in favor of them finding a better home. Your children are precious. It would be best if you could mother them yourself, but sometimes giving them up to a more stable family is the only good choice.

Parenting is a challenge. Try not to do it all by yourself. Whether or not it is possible to have two parents in the home, extended family and church family do much to enrich children's lives. If you do not wish to live with the other parent, do your best to get along with the other parent and to keep him involved. Fathers, your input is vital and shouldn't be limited to child support. More fathers are raising their children as single parents and proving they can do a good job. If the mom isn't providing a healthy environment, reach out to those kids. If you can get custody or shared parenting without taking a combative stance, this will save you a bundle in legal fees. Always speak of the other parent with respect. When you teach them to disrespect the other parent, you are next in line.

All of us fall short as parents. We need to be honest with ourselves so that we can get the help we need to provide our children with safe, healthy homes and loving caregivers. Steps to regain control may be drastic, but they also can be as simple as having a few hours to yourself a week. While most children would be better off with their natural parents, it is the height of selfishness to assume we can do it all by ourselves. Parenting is a team effort.

Chapter 20

Hope is the light by which we stitch and snip and make our comforter. Hope is essential to life. When Jerry's first heart catheterization was scheduled, a friend told me not to worry because it would probably be nothing. I consciously chose to believe. There was nothing we could do to hasten the test or to assure a good outcome. If things were as bad as I thought, I would need my strength for what lay ahead. I chose to accept the offered hope.

In the Bible, we find all the hope we need. We find hope more solid than a friend's assurance that everything will be all right. We know that we will be healed and restored. The process begins here and ends in eternity. As we work hand in hand with God, we gain a greater understanding of all that He is willing to do to help us.

There are many ways to cultivate this friendship with God. I love to listen to Christian music. I enjoy every form it takes, but contemporary Christian music seems to be the best outlet for my emotions. Because most of the lyrics are directed toward God, it contributes to the awareness that He is indeed by our side every moment of every day. We can do nothing so dirty, ugly, or evil as to cause Him to abandon us.

Sin is described as separation from God because it puts blinders on our eyes. When we are deep in sin, He doesn't move. We just can't find Him in the mess we have created. When we cry out in earnest, we discover that He is right there. He never leaves us. He never forsakes us (Hebrews 13:5).

When I was a child, I discovered embroidery. I found such peace and satisfaction in working the pretty thread into a bright, cheerful picture. Back then I worked on pillowcases. Now I embroider anything that doesn't run when I get the needle out. Later, I realized that the peace I felt while embroidering came from God, but I still didn't understand why.

One day after church I showed some of my work to Bud and his wife. She had suggested I get back to embroidery. I found the same satisfaction and peace. It was an easy way to get in touch with God and sooth my nerves. When I told them I didn't understand why the embroidery was so helpful, Bud told me, "Beauty draws us to God."

Train your eye to savor beauty wherever it appears. A purple crocus in the snow, a cheerful dress on a stranger, or a bit of bright blue sky all draw us to God. Do what you can to make your surroundings pretty. Sometimes I've posted National Geographic photos on my wooden doors with transparent tape. Since I don't like to paint walls, I prefer to hang pictures to beautify the space. A plastic tablecloth is a quick way to spruce up an ugly table or dresser top. Contact paper can transform a tomato box into something special. God will see to it that you find beauty that fits your budget.

Do all you can to remind yourself that He is rooting for you. As you improve inch by inch, He remains with you. He lifts you up and He comforts you when you slide downhill in the mud. Patiently He cleans you up. Carefully He dresses your wounds. With infinite tenderness He leads you back up the hill. God will never give up on you. It is okay to rest. You don't have to be constantly slugging away at improving yourself. Ask God to order your days, and He will tell you when to get up and work on climbing that hill. I will tell you a secret: As long as we draw breath, we will never quite get to the top.

Our most important effort is to hear His voice as one eager to heed His advice. He will clear up the confusion. He will light the darkness.

When you cannot restore what you have broken, He will work on it. He never sleeps. He never takes a day off. Because He is infinite, He can listen to you as if there is no one else in the universe that needs Him. Things will get better. Just let God shoulder the load.

We invite you to view the complete
selection of titles we publish at:

www.TEACHServices.com

Scan with your mobile
device to go directly
to our website.

Please write or email us your praises, reactions, or
thoughts about this or any other book we publish at:

TEACH Services, Inc.
P U B L I S H I N G
www.TEACHServices.com ● (800) 367-1844

P.O. Box 954
Ringgold, GA 30736

info@TEACHServices.com

TEACH Services, Inc., titles may be purchased in bulk for
educational, business, fund-raising, or sales promotional use.
For information, please e-mail:

BulkSales@TEACHServices.com

Finally, if you are interested in seeing
your own book in print, please contact us at

publishing@TEACHServices.com

We would be happy to review your manuscript for free.

CPSIA information can be obtained at www.ICGtesting.com
Printed in the USA
LVOW01s0847120615

442239LV00004B/5/P